"Success doesn't just happen. Michael Hyatt and Daniel Harkavy show you how to develop and utilize a clear and compelling Life Plan to create the life you want and truly deserve."

TONY ROBBINS, *New York Times* bestselling author; CEO, Anthony Robbins Companies

"A step-by-step approach to one of life's greatest challenges. If you feel stuck, you probably are, and *Living Forward* might be exactly what you need."

SETH GODIN, author, *What to Do When It's Your Turn*

"An intelligent and articulate manual. Applying even a portion of its simple and practical recommendations will improve anyone's condition in life."

DAVID ALLEN, *New York Times* bestselling author, *Getting Things Done*

"What makes this book special is the authors' passion not just to share a formula but to actually lead readers through the process of prioritizing the time it takes to create and execute their plan."

CHALENE JOHNSON, *New York Times* bestselling author; CEO, Team Johnson

"I've been studying successful people for over twenty years. What I've seen time and again is that success starts with a plan. Michael Hyatt and Daniel Harkavy show us how to craft a plan for our lives so we can experience the success we desire."

DARREN HARDY, *New York Times* bestselling author, *The Compound Effect*; publisher, *Success*

"An extremely practical and undeniably necessary guide for any adult who has drifted from how they thought life should be lived. I have benefited from this approach in my own life."

PATRICK LENCIONI, president, The Table Group; author, *The Advantage*

"This book is a must-read—full of reminders and revelations that will open up your mind and organize your time."

DAVE RAMSEY, *New York Times* bestselling author, *The Total Money Makeover*

"You can either intentionally pursue the essential or you can unintentionally drift into the nonessential. This book brilliantly teaches how to do the former while avoiding the latter."

    GREG MCKEOWN, *New York Times* bestselling author, *Essentialism*

"Many people talk about the importance of having a plan for your life, but no one could really tell you how to create one. Until now."

    JOHN C. MAXWELL, *New York Times* bestselling author; founder, The John Maxwell Company

"It's more than a book, it's a road map to help you get from where you are to where you want to go."

    JON GORDON, *New York Times* bestselling author, *The Energy Bus*

"Michael Hyatt and Daniel Harkavy have much to teach us. May we learn from them the power of living on purpose."

    MAX LUCADO, *New York Times* bestselling author, *Fearless* and *Outlive Your Life*

"Successful people not only launch well, they live well. And that takes more than luck or even hard work. It takes intentionality and a crystal-clear vision for where you are going. *Living Forward* shows you how to design a great life and then chart a course to that life."

    JEFF WALKER, *New York Times* bestselling author, *Launch*; creator, Product Launch Formula

"I know of very few people who have accomplished as much as these two and survived to enjoy their achievements. This is a plan I can get behind."

    DONALD MILLER, *New York Times* bestselling author; founder and CEO, StoryBrand

"Would you start a business, a building, or a battle without a plan? Then why do most of us live our lives without one? *Living Forward* offers a powerful and effective life-planning model that will enable you attain the success in life you deserve."

    BOB GOFF, *New York Times* bestselling author, *Love Does*

"If you apply even 10 percent of the advice contained in this book, your life will be changed forever."

CHRIS GUILLEBEAU, *New York Times* bestselling author, *The $100 Startup*

"Plans and purpose are the mechanics of what you'll learn in *Living Forward*. Hyatt and Harkavy's ideas and insights will drive you forward into action, and that's what matters."

CHRIS BROGAN, *New York Times* bestselling author, *Insider*

"One of the biggest accelerators to change is simplicity. I love how Michael and Daniel have made life planning simple. This guide will help keep you focused and moving forward."

DR. HENRY CLOUD, *New York Times* bestselling author, *Boundaries* and *Necessary Endings*

"A brilliant and motivating resource that will equip you to stop sleepwalking through life and intentionally pursue the plan God has for you."

LYSA TERKEURST, *New York Times* bestselling author; president, Proverbs 31 Ministries

"Success starts with a plan. And Michael Hyatt and Daniel Harkavy remind us that includes planning for a successful life."

FAWN WEAVER, *New York Times* bestselling author, *The Argument-Free Marriage*; founder, The Happy Wives Club

"The real American Dream is to live a life of purpose and meaning, evidenced by physical, emotional, spiritual, and relational abundance. This book will move you from 'I wish' to 'I did.'"

DAN MILLER, *New York Times* bestselling author, *48 Days to the Work You Love*

"If I had a time machine, I would go back to the twenty-two-year-old me and hand him this book. I'd beg him to read it and then dare him to actually put the excellent principles into practice."

JON ACUFF, *New York Times* bestselling author, *Do Over* and *Start*

"You don't have to keep living life spinning your wheels, exhausting yourself, and getting nowhere! This book provides the tools and step-by-step help to clarify where you want to go in life."

CRYSTAL PAINE, *New York Times* bestselling author; founder, MoneySavingMom.com

"With *Living Forward*, Michael Hyatt and Daniel Harkavy have fired a laser beam of focus into a world of uncertainty. Finally, a brightly lit, well-marked pathway for the person who desires true and lasting success!"

ANDY ANDREWS, *New York Times* bestselling author, *The Traveler's Gift* and *The Noticer*

"I've planned all of my life, but this system brings my priorities into focus and keeps me in present-day reality while my gaze is on the future. Thanks, Michael and Daniel, for a fun and creative book!"

STEVE ARTERBURN, *New York Times* bestselling author, *Healing Is a Choice*

"Here's the test of any message: Does the author practice what he preaches? I've seen Michael and Daniel live this message for years with integrity. They have earned the right to speak, and we'll all benefit from listening!"

JOHN ELDREDGE, *New York Times* bestselling author, *Wild at Heart* and *Beautiful Outlaw*

"Everybody ends up somewhere in life. Blessed are those who end up somewhere on purpose! If you lean toward the purpose side of the equation, then I would highly recommend *Living Forward*."

ANDY STANLEY, senior pastor, North Point Community Church; author, *The Next*

"Life is too short to let it go by without being intentional. In *Living Forward*, Michael and Daniel help us discover a purposeful plan to live the life we know we deserve."

PAT FLYNN, podcaster, *Smart Passive Income*

"It's hard to make conscious changes in your life, but it's so much easier when you have a plan. And I can't think of anyone better to help you make that plan than Michael and Daniel."

ALLISON VESTERFELT, author, *Packing Light*

"Michael Hyatt and Daniel Harkavy are the gatekeepers to unlocking your purpose, and this book is the key to having an extraordinary life."

LEWIS HOWES, entrepreneur; author, *The School of Greatness*

"I thought I was skeptical about life planning—until I read this book. This is quite simply the best process for designing a well-lived life that I have ever read."

JEFF GOINS, author, *The Art of Work*

"New insight into the power of purpose, discovering your dreams, and turning your desires into reality."

DR. JOSH AXE, founder, DrAxe.com

"Are you living with good intentions rather than intentionally living? If so, stop now. Let *Living Forward* guide where you want to be. Then, breathe easy."

MICHAEL STELZNER, founder, Social Media Examiner; author, *Launch*

"Without structure in life, we drift. Michael and Daniel acknowledge this reality in chapter 1 and proceed to lay out a structure that supports living a life of intention, focus, and enjoyment."

JOHN LEE DUMAS, host, *EntrepreneurOnFire* podcast; author, *Podcast Launch*

"Throughout the pages of *Living Forward*, Michael Hyatt and Daniel Harkavy take you by the hand and enable you to be the pilot in your flight of life. Pick up a copy, take action, and enjoy your life like never before!"

CHRIS DUCKER, serial entrepreneur and virtual CEO; author of *Virtual Freedom*

"Michael and Daniel are wise guides toward a way of living with intention and purpose, no matter your season of life."

SHAUNA NIEQUIST, author, *Bread & Wine* and *Savor*

"If you're already counting each day as a chance to take another meaningful step toward achieving your ultimate purpose, *Living Forward* will give you a powerful road map for creating a lasting legacy."

ROBERT D. SMITH, author, *20,000 Days and Counting*

"It's easy to drift and find yourself living a life you're not excited about. Michael and Daniel's book helps you uncover your life's purpose and create a plan for living it."

ANDREW WARNER, founder, Mixergy.com

"The power of *Living Forward* lies in the elegant simplicity of the book—it is a short book with a long and lasting impact. Using this book you can create your own Life Plan in a single day, and quite literally change the course of your life."

RAY EDWARDS, host, *The Ray Edwards Show*; founder, Ray Edwards International

"As a busy entrepreneur, I'm always looking for a simple, proven system for achieving my goals. If only there were a system like this for daily life. Thanks to Michael Hyatt and Daniel Harkavy, now there is one!"

AMY PORTERFIELD, creator, The Profit Lab

"Michael Hyatt fascinates me. I'm not even in the same industry, but I'm constantly taking cues and learning from everything he does. And now he has a full life plan with *Living Forward*? Sold. No-brainer."

JEREMY COWART, celebrity photographer; founder, SeeUniversity.com

"Because of the life-planning process, I'm a better wife, mother, daughter, friend, and colleague. I'm grateful to have had the opportunity to benefit from the concepts in this book early in my career."

AMY HIETT, general manager, The Table Group

"*Living Forward* is a must-read. It's a refinement of a life-planning process originally conceived by Daniel Harkavy, who has helped thousands of professional men and women live life more intentionally."

JERRY BAKER, former CEO, First Tennessee Bank and First Horizon Home Loans

"How tragic to spend a life with no purpose or end in mind. *Living Forward* is a great tool to either get you started down the right road or to make sure you are still on that road."

RON BLUE, founder, Ronald Blue & Company; author, *Master Your Money*

"Many of us go through life unfocused and unable to confidently set the 'big, hairy, audacious' goals that God wants us to pursue. Thankfully, Hyatt and Harkavy have developed this unique and powerful planning system to help take us to proactively living a rich life of meaning and significance."

DAN T. CATHY, president and chief operating officer, Chick-fil-A, Inc.

"In our busy world we tend to plan for everything except for what is the most important—our life. Daniel Harkavy and Michael Hyatt give us a very pragmatic tool to define what we want our life to be, to create a plan, and to stick to it."

DOMINIQUE FOURNIER, former CEO, Infineum International Limited

"A toolkit of wisdom to create the professional and personal life you have envisioned for yourself."

TREVOR GRAVES, founder, Nemo Design

"*Living Forward* is a remarkable gift that provides me the tools and easy-to-follow processes to define my purpose and build a legacy that will add value to my family, co-workers, and friends."

MARC LAIRD, chairman and CEO, Cornerstone Home Lending

"Prior to *Living Forward*, people interested in learning this process would have had to spend thousands of dollars engaging an executive coach. Daniel and Michael have codified the process and put it into an individually digestible medium for all to benefit from."

CORY MAHAFFEY, managing partner, Northwestern Mutual

"*Living Forward* can be utilized by anyone from the busy executive needing to regain perspective to the college graduate starting a new job. Every page is full of wisdom and advice born from experience."

DAVID "SKIP" PRICHARD, president and CEO, OCLC

"I made Harkavy and Hyatt's process a part of my life several years ago, as did numerous members of our leadership team, and I promise you it is a game changer!"

TODD SALMANS, CEO, PrimeLending

"We only get one life to live on this earth, and as a result, this life should be filled with purpose and positive impact. Daniel and Michael's life-planning process is real. It will help you be your best for your best."

MARTIN WHALEN, vice president, Essilor USA

"I loved the several levels of *Living Forward*: the philosophical level (thinking about the purpose of my life), the strategic level (how to structure my life), the tactical level (how to set up a plan), and the practical level (how to go forward step by step)."

MARTIN DAUM, president and CEO, Daimler Trucks North America

"This is authentic coaching—a facilitated exploration to help discern and respond to God's call on our lives. It will be required reading at the Institute."

CHRISTOPHER MCCLUSKEY, president, Professional Christian Coaching Institute; founder, ChristianLifeCoaching.com

LIVING FORWARD

A PROVEN PLAN *to* STOP DRIFTING *and* GET *the* LIFE YOU WANT

MICHAEL HYATT *and* DANIEL HARKAVY

BakerBooks

a division of Baker Publishing Group
Grand Rapids, Michigan

© 2016 by Michael Hyatt and Daniel Harkavy

Published by Baker Books
a division of Baker Publishing Group
P.O. Box 6287, Grand Rapids, MI 49516-6287
www.bakerbooks.com

Printed in the United States of America

Library of Congress Cataloging-in-Publication Data is on file at the Library of Congress, Washington, DC.

ISBN 978-0-8010-1882-4
ISBN 978-0-8010-1884-8 (ITPE)

Scripture quotations labeled NASB are from the New American Standard Bible®, copyright © 1960, 1962, 1963, 1968, 1971, 1972, 1973, 1975, 1977, 1995 by The Lockman Foundation. Used by permission. (www.Lockman.org)

Scripture quotations labeled NIV are from the Holy Bible, New International Version®. NIV®. Copyright © 1973, 1978, 1984, 2011 by Biblica, Inc.™ Used by permission of Zondervan. All rights reserved worldwide. www.zondervan.com

To protect the privacy of those referenced in this book, in most cases names and details have been changed.

Authors are represented by Alive Literary Agency, 7680 Goddard Street, Suite 200, Colorado Springs, CO 80920, www.aliveliterary.com.

16 17 18 19 20 21 22   7 6 5 4 3 2 1

To our beautiful brides, Gail and Sheri,
and to our wonderful kids!
You fill our lives with love, adventure,
and true companionship.

Contents

Introduction

An App for Your Life

The first step towards getting somewhere is to decide you're not going to stay where you are.

—John Pierpont "J.P." Morgan

It was a beautiful July morning, and I (Michael) was hiking deep in the Colorado Rockies. The trail ran along a gurgling stream. Wildflowers were in bloom and the air was sweet with the scent of pine trees, cottonwoods, and rich earth. The temperature was a cool 64 degrees—perfect for a long hike. Arriving at the first milestone, a familiar footbridge over the stream, I paused to take it all in, totally lost in the experience.

Soon I took a second footbridge back across the stream and followed the trail away from it. Another ten minutes of steep uphill hiking, and I came to a dry creek bed that went almost straight up. A little winded at this point, I decided I'd gone far enough, sipped a little water, and started back down. After crossing the second footbridge back over the stream, I kept on the same downward trail—or so I thought. Strangely, I could no longer hear the stream. The forest was now darker and denser than I'd remembered. It took a moment, but it dawned on me that I was more than lost in the experience. I was actually lost! Somewhere along the way I'd taken a wrong turn and ended up on another trail.

I was, thankfully, using an iPhone exercise app that tracked my path. I pulled out my phone and prayed for a signal. Yes! Five bars. My path was traced on the map so I could see where I had started and every turn I'd taken along the way—including the wrong turn. In less than ten minutes I was back on the right path.

An App for Your Life

A mountain hike is one thing. Daily life is different. If you find yourself off course, you can't simply open a GPS app for your life. Or can you?

Whenever we use the term *Life Planning*, people get it. Whether we're talking about it in a speech, coaching session, blog post, or casual conversation, just about everyone recognizes the value of the concept—even if they've never really considered it before.

- Maybe it's because as they look around, they see a lot of unhappy people who don't have a clue how they ended up where they are.
- Maybe it's because deep down inside, they know they're drifting through life with no clear direction.

- Maybe it's because life is more complicated than they had initially thought, and they know they need a map.
- Maybe it's because life is not turning out like they had hoped, and they are ready to get things back on track.
- Maybe it's because they are in their forties, fifties, or sixties and cannot believe how fast the years have flown by.
- Maybe it's because the story of their life is good at this point, but they are aware of their limited time and want to ensure they live an even better story.

If this describes you, you have picked up the right book. A Life Plan is the app you need to stay on the path to the life you desire. Without a plan, chances are good you'll end up at an unintended destination: an unhappy marriage, an unfulfilling career, in bad health, or all of the above.

Most of us see the inherent wisdom of planning. We may plan for next year's vacation, our children's college education, or our own retirement. But for some strange reason, it never occurs to us to plan our lives. It didn't occur to the two of us at first either. But then we saw what we were missing.

Wake-Up Call

At age twenty I (Daniel) started my career in the mortgage industry. At twenty-three I was promoted to a management position. Over the next few years, the company grew from eight to seventeen branches. With a lot of hard work, I was able to attract and develop a winning team which led us to a rapid accent to the top performing branch.

At twenty-eight I was promoted to a vice president position over all our branches. I oversaw two hundred loan originators and leaders throughout California, Oregon, Washington, and Nevada. And that's when things got tricky. The CEO of the company was a mentor and friend. He said he was grooming me to take his seat. The company had gone public the previous year, and the future looked incredibly bright. I was far exceeding my financial goals and couldn't imagine a better plan for my career.

But I sensed deep down that something was off. Many of my peers in the industry were wealthy by most standards, but many of them paid heavy prices for their success. Some were divorced or complained of unfulfilling marriages. Some had very challenging relationships with their teens who wound up in real trouble. Some could not make it through a day without the aid of a cocktail or drug. Few invested in their physical and spiritual well-being. As I looked around at many of the faster-paced industries, I saw some of the same trends.

At this stage of life—married with three little kids—I could see my life heading down the wrong path. These people were highly successful in one area of their lives—money—yet bankrupt in areas that mattered most. I wasn't judging, but I didn't like what I saw and knew a major change was needed to write a different story for myself. I thought long and hard about the path I was on.

As I reconsidered things, my definition of success began to change. What previously motivated me lost its attraction. I was no longer about income, possessions, or title. I wanted more but was unsure what I wanted more of. So I quit. It made no sense to some, but it made complete sense to me.

I decided to take a one-year sabbatical. During that time I explored the options for my next career and settled on starting a business-coaching company, which became Building

Champions, Inc. This is also when I was first introduced to the concept of Life Planning. I had become friends with author and sales trainer Todd Duncan. He played an instrumental role in helping me launch this new business, and Life Planning was a process he used in his training.

During my sabbatical I wrote my first Life Plan and later created the tool that is the foundation for this book. Believing that self-leadership always precedes team leadership, we start our clients with Life Planning before discussing business and leadership development. Over the years thousands have been helped by the Life Planning process.

Life Planning has been a big help to me too. More than twenty years after discovering and implementing the process, I not only avoided the fate of some of my colleagues, I've been able to structure my days around the things that matter most.

Michael's story is similar.

The Cost of Success

In July of 2000 the publisher of Nelson Books, one of the imprints of Thomas Nelson Publishers, suddenly resigned. I (Michael) was asked to fill the job and became responsible for the business. The division was in bad shape, that much I knew, but I had no idea just how bad. As it turns out, Nelson Books was the least profitable division in a company of fourteen divisions.

Over the next eighteen months I did very little other than work to turn things around. I was constantly on the road, and my team and I spent innumerable evenings at the office. We went from being the least profitable division to the most profitable. I was promoted again and given additional responsibilities.

But success began to take its toll. As the workload increased, exercise decreased. I ate more and more junk food and began to gain weight. I felt stressed and eventually ended up in the emergency room with what I thought was a heart attack. Thankfully it wasn't—just the worst case of acid reflux ever. But it scared me to death and got my attention. I realized that while I had a plan for my career, I didn't have one for my life. If something didn't change, I was going to burn out, break down, or worse.

On the recommendation of a friend, I hired Daniel as my executive coach. "Life doesn't have to be this way," he encouraged me. It could be lived with purpose and balance. To show how, Daniel helped me create a Life Plan. It was the first time I had ever systematically thought about what outcomes I wanted to see in the major areas of my life outside work. For the first time in months, I started to hope.

"This won't insulate you from life's adversities and unexpected turns," Daniel warned, "but it will help you become an active participant in your life, intentionally shaping your own future." He was right. The experience of creating a Life Plan, regularly reviewing it, and updating it as necessary, has been transformational for us both. As our family, friends, career, and other interests have grown, our Life Plans have kept us on track, holding true to the things we value most.

It's from our own experience that we want to share with you the power of creating a Life Plan. Here's the great news. You don't have to be a middle-aged executive on the verge of burnout to benefit from Life Planning. In fact, the earlier you get started, the more influence you can have on getting the life you want—financially, relationally, physically, and spiritually. People at any stage will profit by taking the wheel and getting pointed in the right direction.

Our Promise to You

All of us get lost from time to time. We think we know the right direction, but we drift off the path. We may not be sure how to get back on track. Or maybe we know exactly where we're going, but we don't like the destination!

In this book we want to provide the clarity you need to articulate a vision for your life—your whole life—and develop a plan for getting to a better destination. It's all about being fully awake to the realities of our personal and professional worlds and using that fresh level of awareness to make better decisions and tell better stories with our lives.

Living Forward will heighten your sense of what's truly possible for you in life. If you feel out of balance, aware that your current pace is unsustainable; if you are making great gains professionally but don't want to neglect personal priorities; if you want to have better focus to succeed financially; if you have gone through a recent tragedy and suddenly become aware that life is short; if any of those are true, this book is for you.

Living Forward will equip you to make better decisions in every area of your life. The good news is that we have more control than most of us realize. Each day is filled with thousands of opportunities to change the story of our lives. We want to help you make the most proactive, intentional, and beneficial decisions possible.

Finally, *Living Forward* will position you to make the most significant contribution in this world that you can and add the most value to those around you.

It takes definitive action to see positive gains. Our goal is to get you in motion, so you can experience the change you want. In this book we will be continuously calling you to action. We have coached individuals in every kind of life circumstance through this process and have seen remarkable transformation. All that matters—and this is critical—is that you are *ready for a positive change.*

What J.P. Morgan said is right: "The first step towards getting somewhere is to decide you're not going to stay where you are."

So let's move forward.

Overview of the Book

Living Forward consists of ten chapters that take you on a journey through realizing your need for a Life Plan, the process of creating one, and the encouragement to make it happen. It's all about equipping you to fill your days with the decisions that enable you to live a more proactive and intentional life. If you choose to follow our recommendations, you will have the tools and know-how to live life looking forward, not out of the rearview mirror. Here's a road map for *Living Forward.*

Chapter 1: *Acknowledge the Drift.* We explore why so few people plan their lives and what happens when they don't. It usually comes down to what we call "the drift," a metaphor for understanding how we arrive at destinations we don't consciously choose. If there's a villain in the story, this is it.

Chapter 2: *Understand the Mission.* We define exactly what we mean by the term *Life Plan,* what it is and isn't. We also share three powerful questions you can use to organize your plan—and your *life.*

Chapter 3: *Appreciate the Benefits.* We elaborate on the six major benefits of creating your Life Plan. It is important to connect with your *why* if you are going to make the effort to create and implement a Life Plan.

Chapter 4: *Design Your Legacy*. We encourage you to fast-forward to the end of your life and ask this question: "What will family, friends, and colleagues say when I am dead?" It might sound morbid, but it's extremely useful. When you are gone, the only truly important thing you will leave behind are the *memories* you've created. How do you want to be remembered? The possibility of shaping those memories can be a powerful lever for motivating positive change.

Chapter 5: *Determine Your Priorities*. We help you identify your various "Life Accounts." And we share an online assessment tool called the Life Assessment Profile™ designed to reveal your *passion* and *progress* in each of these nine major domains of life.

Chapter 6: *Chart the Course*. Once you have determined your priorities, it is time to create an "Action Plan" for each account. This is where you think through where you are and where you want to be. We help you create a purpose statement, describe your envisioned future, determine your current reality, and craft specific commitments.

Chapter 7: *Dedicate One Day*. By the time you get to this chapter, you will have all the tools necessary to create a Life Plan. Now—and not later—is the time to create it. We explain the value of scheduling a full day, how to prepare for it, and how to get it done.

Chapter 8: *Implement Your Plan*. This is where the rubber meets the road. The goal of Life Planning is to change your life and get you on the path to the life you've always dreamed of having. The key is margin—the time and energy to adopt new practices and achieve your results. We share three strategies for creating the margin you need to make the progress you want.

Chapter 9: *Keep It Alive.* A Life Plan is worthless unless you review it on a regular basis. We suggest a pattern of regular review—weekly, quarterly, yearly—and provide an agenda and resources for each. Based on our extensive experience coaching thousands of clients and seminar attendees, regular review and revision are crucial for making your Life Plan a living and effective document.

Chapter 10: *Join the Revolution.* Smart organizations encourage their employees to develop Life Plans. We explain why and how you can implement Life Planning in your organization—even if you aren't the CEO. The payoff will be more productive and engaged employees, creating a culture with a strategic advantage in today's competitive environment.

In addition to these chapters, we provide four sample Life Plans from people from a variety of life circumstances. These—along with a series of nut-and-bolt resources you can access at LivingForwardBook.com—show you how it all comes together in a single document.

The Journey Begins

We are grateful that you have chosen to read this book, and we are confident you can live a better story if you fully engage with the ideas and processes that follow.

Living Forward will resonate with those who want the peace that comes from knowing what matters most to them and how to fill their days, weeks, months, and years with actions that will enable them to make the greatest difference possible.

This could be more than the beginning of a book. It just might be the beginning of a transformed life—a life of purpose and intention. The change begins *now.*

Part One

UNDERSTAND YOUR NEED

1

Acknowledge the Drift

To reach a port we must sail, sometimes with the wind, and
sometimes against it. But we must not drift or lie at anchor.

—Oliver Wendell Holmes

I (Daniel) have a little cabin on the Oregon coast. The beaches
of the Northwest are gorgeous and filled with some challenging and fantastic surf. During the fall and winter months,
storms roll in and produce very large, clean waves. Unfortunately, the waves will sometimes surge with heavy winds and
currents that can cause absolute chaos in the water.

It was one of those days. The waves were breaking toward
the end of a nearby cape that juts more than a hundred yards
into the ocean. I paddled out with three others, including
Austin, who was new to surfing. Not long after making our
way out, I noticed Austin was being swept past the cape to
the sea. He was stuck in a very strong riptide.

Austin was strong but lacked the water knowledge to get out of the current. It just kept pulling him farther along. I paddled to the edge of the rip and then toward him with the current. When I caught up, I directed Austin to change course. Instead of paddling toward the shore, which seemed to make sense, we paddled parallel to it. If we went far enough, I knew we would be out of the rip and in calmer waters. Then we would be free to paddle toward shore. It took half an hour, but we finally made our way back to the sand, exhausted.

Life can have the same effect on us. It is so easy for us to find ourselves stuck in a riptide and pulled off course. Worse, we can find ourselves in harm's way. Many people get into their forties, fifties, and sixties, look around, and realize they have been pulled out to sea. Perhaps their health is failing, their marriage is broken, or their career is stalled. Maybe they have lost their spiritual connection, and life seems meaningless and unfulfilling. Whatever the case, they look up and find themselves far away from where they thought they would be at this point in their lives. They have become victims of the drift.

How Did We End Up Here?

Drifting usually happens for one or more of the following four reasons:

1. *It happens when we are unaware.* Sometimes we drift because we simply don't know what's happening or what's really at stake. This happened in the story above. Austin was new to those particular waters and didn't have any experience with the currents.

This can happen in real life too. Maybe you were raised with assumptions about your health, marriage dynamics, or work that are simply unhelpful. We all have ideas about life that are inaccurate. Until we see differently, we just don't know.

2. *It happens when we are distracted.* I (Michael) once got caught in a riptide as well. Vacationing with my wife, Gail, in Hawaii, we took a boogie board out snorkeling. The underwater sights were amazing, but we were so distracted we forgot to keep track of the shore. When we finally looked up and around, we were hundreds of yards out to sea and had to swim for our lives to make it back!

Perhaps you're caught up in your career and find it more interesting than spending time with your family. Or maybe you're in a particularly busy season of parenting and neglecting your health. Maybe you're so enamored with apps and gadgets, you're not getting the work done that you were hired to do.

3. *It happens when we are overwhelmed.* Sometimes we take on more than we should. Sometimes we are given more than we think we can bear. Regardless, we feel swamped. To relieve the problem, we convince ourselves the situation is temporary. "We will give full attention to [fill in the blank] as soon as we get through this season," we promise ourselves and others.

Occasionally this is legit, but it's usually an excuse. This is especially true when we drift from one overwhelming situation to another, with no real attempt to stop and ask, "Why do I keep ending up in these situations?"

4. *It happens when we are deceived.* It's amazing how our minds work. We're often unconscious about the relationship between our beliefs and reality. "Whether you believe you can

do a thing or not, you are right," said Henry Ford. In other words, what we believe about something often creates the outcome we experience.

This is especially relevant to the drift. Perhaps you think *you* can't change. Or *they* won't change. Or *the world* won't change. You refuse to accept the fact that you have *control* and can affect the outcome. As a result, you drift, feeling powerless to change course.

The Consequences of Drifting

Drifting can have serious consequences, not only for you, but for those you love and those counting on you. In some situations drifting can be flat-out dangerous. It's important to understand the consequences so you can avoid the problem and take corrective action now—while you still can avoid one or more of these five costly consequences:

1. *Confusion.* When we are drifting, we lose perspective. Without a clear destination in view, the challenges on the journey seem pointless. There's no larger story to provide meaning to life's smaller dramas. When this happens, we get disoriented. Like a hiker without a compass or GPS, we walk in circles, lost in a forest of unrelated events and activities. We eventually wonder if our life has any meaning and despair of finding purpose.

2. *Expense.* Drifting through life can also be enormously expensive, both in terms of money and—more importantly—time. Too often we zigzag our way through life, uncertain of the destination and eating up valuable and finite resources. Sometimes the best thing you can do is stop and get your bearings. While doing so may seem

to delay the journey, ultimately it is faster and cheaper in terms of getting where you really want to go.

3. *Lost opportunity.* Unless we have a destination in mind, it's tough to separate the opportunities from the distractions. *Will this situation move me closer to my goal or further away?* we ask. Without a plan, we have no way of knowing. There's no real sense of urgency, no reason to seize the opportunity, and no sense that we might lose it if we don't. Then it's easy to procrastinate. And most opportunities have expiration dates. If missed, they are often lost forever.

4. *Pain.* While some pain in life is unavoidable, we bring much of it on ourselves. Too often this is simply because we failed to plan. For example,

- Without a plan for our health, whether physical, mental, or spiritual, we can end up sick, without energy, stuck in the doldrums, or . . . dead!

- Without a plan for our career, we can end up unfulfilled, stalled, or unemployed.

- Without a plan for our marriage, we can end up miserable, separated, or divorced.

- Without a plan for our parenting, we can end up with estranged relationships, damaged kids, and real regrets.

This is the danger of drifting. If we attempt life's journey without a plan, we can find ourselves in trouble—perhaps deep trouble—fast.

5. *Regrets.* Perhaps the saddest consequence of all is getting to the end of life with deep regrets. We experience the "if onlys":

If only I had eaten better, exercised more, and taken better care of my body.

If only I had spent more time reading, learning another language, or visiting other countries.

If only I had spent more time trying to connect with my spouse, listening rather than talking, and seeking to understand rather than being understood.

If only I had spent more time with my children—going to their games and recitals, taking them camping and fishing, and explaining how to navigate life.

If only I had been brave enough to launch out and start my own business.

If only I had been more generous, giving of my time, talent, and money, trying to help those who needed a hand.

We all know the truth of the adage "Life is not a dress rehearsal." There are real consequences to getting it wrong. Many of us are working our way through those consequences now. There's no way around it—we live in the aftermath of our choices. But the good news is, our decisions are the one thing we can control. Today's the day to make those choices really count.

A Preview of the Process

Life Planning is the exact opposite of the drift. The drift is about passivity. Life Planning is about proactivity. The drift is about blaming our circumstances or other people. Life Planning is about taking responsibility. The drift is about living without a plan. Life Planning is about having a plan and working it.

This book is organized according to three goals we want to help you accomplish:

1. *Become aware of your current location.* We want to help you see where you are in relation to where you want to be. Fully acknowledging your current reality in every area of your life is critical to going in a better direction. We'll cover this in chapters 2–3.

2. *Decide where you want to go.* The essence of Life Planning is envisioning a better future. We want to empower you to dream. What kind of physical, mental, or spiritual health do you want to possess? What kind of marriage do you want to enjoy? What kind of career do you want to have? Why settle for drifting to a boring—or even dangerous—situation? We'll cover this in chapters 4–7 and provide you with some simple but powerful tools and templates to help you chart your desired course.

3. *Start working toward your destination.* Once you have acknowledged where you are and decided where you want to go, you can begin moving toward your goals. Yes, it will take work. But you are now aware of the gap and can begin filling your day with the actions that will close it. When you have a plan, every day becomes an opportunity to move toward your destination. We'll cover this in chapters 8–10.

Wherever you are, hear us: You may feel that you've drifted too far off course to get back on track, like the shore is just too far away. Perhaps you have given up hope and don't believe things can ever be different. This is simply not true. It's never too late. Be encouraged. You can't change the past, but all of us have the power to change the future. The right choices today will radically alter the shape of tomorrow.

2

Understand the Mission

Make no little plans; they have no magic to stir men's blood
and probably will themselves not be realized. Make big plans;
aim high in hope and work, remembering that a noble, logi-
cal diagram once recorded will not die.

—Daniel H. Burnham

Benjamin Franklin is the first Life Planner we know of.
Around 1730, while in his late twenties, he drafted a plan
for self-improvement. He listed thirteen essential virtues he
wanted to develop in his life—things like temperance, fru-
gality, industry, and humility. He chose one virtue to focus
on each week and kept a daily chart to track his progress.[1]

Challenging as it was, Franklin's plan was relatively simple.
But the first time I (Michael) heard about Life Planning, I
thought it might be like corporate strategic planning, only
more detailed—a three-ring binder with a detailed SWOT[2]

analysis, action plans, and Gantt charts. Who's got time for that?

What Is a Life Plan?

While others have written or spoken on this topic as well, the term *Life Plan* seems to have been commandeered by the financial services industry. If you Google the phrase, 99 percent of the results point to websites selling financial or insurance products. Not us. We are using this phrase to refer to a specific kind of document. When we say Life Plan, here's what we mean:

> A Life Plan is a short written document, usually eight to fifteen pages long. It is created by you and for you. It describes how you want to be remembered. It articulates your personal priorities. It provides the specific actions necessary to take you from where you are to where you want to be in every major area of your life. It is most of all a living document that you will tweak and adjust as necessary for the rest of your life.

Let's unpack this a phrase at a time.

A Life Plan is a short written document, usually five to fifteen pages long. Yes, that's right. Not a big, fat, three-ring binder with a hundred pages of detailed plans. No, just a short, written document that you can read with ease on a daily or weekly basis.

Don't let the brevity fool you. Length does not correlate to impact. The Ten Commandments, Sermon on the Mount, Edict of Milan, Magna Carta, Luther's 95 Theses, Mayflower Compact, Declaration of Independence, United States Constitution, Gettysburg Address, and the Emancipation Proclamation—all of these world-changing documents are less than five thousand words, about fifteen to twenty pages in a printed book. And the majority is fewer than a thousand words, just three to five pages. A text does not have to be long to change the course of history. Nor does your Life Plan have to be long to change the course of *your history.* Eight to fifteen pages is all it takes.

It is created by you and for you. You can't hire someone else to do this for you. This is something that has to start with *you.* It has to flow from your heart. No one else can create it. No one else will likely read it (except perhaps someone who will help you achieve your goals, like a spouse, close friend, or a coach). It is created exclusively by you, for you.

It describes how you want to be remembered. When we are gone, the only essential thing we will leave behind are the memories we *create* in the lives of those we have touched and those we love. The cool thing is that we have the opportunity to engineer those *now.* We don't have to leave them to chance. We can be intentional about creating them.

It articulates your personal priorities. For most of us, our priorities are set by external forces—our spouse, our parents or families, our boss, or our social network. But what are *our* priorities? What are the ones that we want to shape our lives? And what do we want to see in each of these priorities at some point in the future? A Life Plan is an opportunity to define that vision for ourselves.

It provides the specific actions necessary to take you from where you are to where you want to be in every major area of your life. Yes, we will get into repeatable or nonnegotiable actions. But these aren't the kind that the Navy uses to build a submarine or corporations use to introduce a new product. These will be simple and to the point.

It is most of all a living document that you will tweak and adjust as necessary for the rest of your life. This is key. A Life Plan is not a result in and of itself. It is the manifestation of an ongoing process wherein you plan, implement, evaluate—and then do it all over again. The first time you create a Life Plan is the hardest. Because you're starting from scratch, it can feel like inventing the wheel. But once you've done it the first time, you just keep the wheel rolling each year by tweaking and improving.

Asking the Right Questions

The Life Plan format is driven by three powerful questions. But before we share those with you, we want to talk about the incredible power of questions. Our lives are shaped by the questions we ask. Good questions lead to good outcomes. Bad questions lead to bad outcomes.

In 2003, for example, I (Michael) was named president of Thomas Nelson Publishers, the seventh largest book publisher in the United States. It was an extremely busy time with a lot of pressure to perform.

One morning on my way to work, I grabbed my computer in my right hand, a fresh cup of coffee in my left, and headed downstairs to leave for work. Four steps from the bottom I slipped on the carpet. Without a free hand to grab the stair rail, I tumbled flat on my rear on the landing, splashing coffee the whole way down. But the mess was only the beginning.

Already running late with a very busy day ahead, I stood to take care of things and get going. That's when the pain hit. My ankle was broken. My day was scuttled. So were the next ten. I had to have surgery, including a plate and six screws to repair the damage. On top of that I had to wear a therapeutic boot for three months. Far from presidential! This couldn't have happened at a worse time.

At this point I could have asked myself several questions: *Why am I so clumsy? Why does this have to happen now? What did I do to deserve this?* But the problem with these questions is that they are completely unproductive and disempowering. They are natural, of course. Probably even necessary. It's all part of the process of grieving a loss. But ultimately there are better questions.

One of the best questions you can ask when something negative happens is this: *What does this experience make possible?* Do you see the shift? Suddenly, your attention moves from the past—which you can't do a thing about—to the future. In my case, a broken ankle had several positive benefits, including some much-needed rest.

Regardless of the circumstances, the bottom line is this: You can't always choose what happens to you. Accidents and tragedies happen. What you can do is choose how you respond to those situations. One of the best ways to begin is to ask yourself the right questions.

Three Powerful Questions

The same is true when it comes to your Life Plan. It is the result of answering three powerful questions. Let's consider them one at a time.

Question 1: *How do I want to be remembered?* In planning anything, the best place to begin is at the end. What outcome do you want? How do you want the story to end? How do you want to be remembered when you are gone? We will cover legacy in detail in chapter 4, but just know that this is a revolutionary question, one worthy of your best thinking and your deepest reflection.

Question 2: *What matters most?* Maybe you have never given yourself permission to ask this question. For example: You know what's important to your parents. You may know what's important to your spouse. You most certainly know what is important to your boss. But what's important to you? What matters most in your life? This is a question about priorities. No one else can decide what they are for you. You must take responsibility for them yourself. We will have more to say about priorities in chapter 5.

Question 3: *How can I get from here to where I want to be?* If you are going to improve your life and realize your potential, you will have to figure out where you are now; where you want to be; and how you get from one to the other. We will discuss charting your course in chapter 6. For now, we just want you to understand the framework.

A GPS for Your Life

We opened the book by comparing Life Planning to a GPS app that gets you back on track. It's a great metaphor, especially in answering the third question, which is all about getting from where you are to where you want to be.

All metaphors break down at some point. But the GPS metaphor serves to underscore and explain how a Life Plan can work for you.

A GPS requires you to input your destination. Nothing happens until you decide where you want to go. The same is true of a Life Plan. It forces you to determine the outcomes in each of your major life categories. This is the first section in the Life Plan.

A GPS gets you to your destination faster with less hassle. We are both directionally challenged. Without technical help, we get lost quickly. Our iPhone navigation system gets us to our destination without the stress of trying to figure it out ourselves. The same is true of a Life Plan.

A GPS gives you constant feedback on your progress. You always know the street you are on, how far you must travel to the next turn, and how far to your ultimate destination. A Life Plan is similar. It tells you where you are in relation to where you want to go. It provides the context and keeps you oriented.

A GPS helps you get back on track when you lose your way. Even with a GPS you might take the occasional wrong turn. (Boy, we sure have!) But the system never chides you. It simply tells you how to get back on track. Same with a Life Plan. It gives you a reference point, so you can reach your destination.

A GPS reroutes you around roadblocks. It is inevitable that you will encounter obstacles on the way to your destination. A good GPS is able to adjust on the fly and recalculate the route. The same is true of a Life Plan. It provides the flexibility to overcome obstacles and keep moving forward.

A GPS is not always accurate. This is not surprising. It's a challenge for map databases to keep up with all the changes: new roads, closed roads, traffic accidents, etc. The same is true of your Life Plan. You won't always get it right. You must adjust as you encounter reality. A Life Plan gives you a framework for doing that.

A GPS requires an investment. Have you rented a car and had to make the decision about paying extra for the navigation system? Though several apps are now available for free, that investment was worth every penny. A Life Plan is similar. It requires an up-front investment of time and regular review. But the rewards are well worth it in the end.

More Than a Document, a Lifelong Practice

As we mentioned previously, writing a Life Plan for the first time is the most difficult. But it will get easier over time. This is not something you write and stick on the shelf. The goal is not just to produce the document and go back to "business as usual."

The real value is in the constant, never-ending improvement. Life Planning is something you will want to do for the rest of your life. In fact, it will become a way of life.

3

Appreciate the Benefits

The man without a purpose is like a ship without a rudder.

—Thomas Carlyle

For the past two decades I (Daniel) and my team have been coaching some of the most amazing business professionals and leaders around the world. Most are accustomed to creating business plans and have some sort of financial plan for their finances. But very few come to Building Champions with any sort of a plan for their lives.

As we said earlier, most people spend more time planning a one-week vacation than identifying what outcomes they want to see in the major areas of their lives. Is it any surprise when life doesn't turn out the way we want?

This is why we believe everyone—especially leaders—should take the time to create a written Life Plan. Self-leadership always precedes team leadership, and the Life Plan can be one of the most powerful tools to help you best lead yourself. There are at least six benefits to doing so.

Benefit No. 1: Clarifying Priorities

By February 2009 the staircase, the coffee, and the therapeutic boot were ancient history. I (Michael) was now CEO of Thomas Nelson Publishers, and the company was smack dab in the middle of what would come to be called the Great Recession. The book industry, dependent as it was on consumer spending, was particularly hard hit. Publishers, printers, and booksellers were all suffering. Sales dropped by almost 20 percent. The company had already gone through two rounds of layoffs, letting almost a quarter of its employees go. These were dark, difficult times. Every day was a battle.

To add insult to injury, Nelson's owners—who had bought the company at the height of the housing-market bubble that later caused the recession—did not foresee a slump when they prepared their forecasts. Neither did we, the staff. Everyone naively assumed sales and profits would continue to move, as the financial people like to say, "up and to the right." So the company was struggling to meet its debt covenants.

My team and I were under enormous pressure. Every day brought a new set of problems, and none of us had a clue when the economy would improve. We controlled what we could and tried to be as creative as possible, but consumers weren't budging. As the months dragged on, the leadership was frustrated and growing desperate.

I knew I needed a vacation. The constant grind was taking a toll. I needed to get away, reconnect with my wife, Gail, and gain some vital perspective. A little rest wouldn't hurt either.

My pace wasn't sustainable. Thankfully, some friends offered their cabin deep in the Colorado Rockies. The remoteness sounded like the perfect prescription, so Gail and I packed our bags, got on a plane, and looked forward to a week away. I planned to unplug once I left Colorado Springs for the cabin, but when we landed in Dallas for our connection, I switched on my cell phone and began to check email. Almost immediately I noticed a message from my boss, one of the partners of the private equity company that owned Thomas Nelson. *What now?*

The email said he and his colleagues planned to visit Monday and he expected me to be there. My heart sank, and I read Gail the email. "What are you going to do?" she asked before offering to call off the trip and return home. She understood the gravity of the situation.

In that moment of tension, facing the reality of two competing priorities, my Life Plan gave me the clarity I needed. Work wasn't the whole of my life. It was only one category—an important one, but not to the exclusion of everything else, especially if allowing it to dominate would undermine it and the rest.

The answer was obvious. "I'm sorry," I replied to my boss, "but I just landed in Dallas. Gail and I are headed to the mountains for a much-needed week of vacation. We need to try and find an alternative time for your visit." It wasn't an easy decision, but I didn't wrestle with it. He wasn't happy, but at that point I knew what I needed to do. My Life Plan gave me the direction and framework I needed to make the call.

We've heard similar stories over and over from the people we've coached. "I'm more confident in *me* now," Philip told us. "Before Life Planning, I would either overanalyze everything, or constantly second-guess the decision itself." It took a while for his priorities to really become second nature once he began Life Planning, but now, he says, "decisions come naturally."

We're confident it will work the same for you. A Life Plan will enable you to set your priorities and understand how they work together—and when they don't.

Benefit No. 2: Maintaining Balance

I (Daniel) was given the opportunity to build and lead my first team weeks before turning twenty-three. I had one month of marriage under my belt as I entered into this new chapter of life. My leadership and management experience at the time was minimal. So my strategy was to be the hardest worker on the team, to find people who wanted to further succeed, and to then help them identify the steps, systems, and knowledge required to reach their goals.

This is when I developed my coaching leadership style that led to starting Building Champions about eight years later. I wish I could say I was smart enough to have crafted this strategy in advance of some pretty heavy sacrifices, but that was not so. As I did all I could to outproduce members of my team (or "lead by example," as I thought), to recruit, develop, and then support the talent that I had attracted, I found that there were not enough hours in a day. I took pride in my levels of service and my availability. My pager gave the world 24/7 access to me.

I can recall a dinner date with my bride at a nice restaurant in Los Angeles during this season and having my pager buzzing constantly. To make matters worse—far, far worse—I actually got up from the table to find a pay phone and respond to everyone pushing my buttons. Talk about ruining a romantic evening! I was completely out of balance and knew that something needed to change.

Many people find themselves in similar circumstances. Some, for example, sacrifice their health for their overloaded schedule. They're too busy to exercise regularly. They choose fast food for fast times, put on weight, and race toward a major health crisis. Others sacrifice their marriage and kids for their career, hobbies, or volunteer work. This doesn't happen all at once, of course. It's incremental. But we start to teeter, lose our balance, and fall—hard sometimes.

I was so motivated to succeed that I was putting all of my energy into my career and believing the lie that this is what is required to succeed. What I knew was that, yes, I would earn more respect, more accolades, and more money, but if my decisions and boundaries did not change, my marriage, my health, and much more would suffer. I needed a solid plan for my life that would help me identify how I could succeed in all of the important areas of my life—not just my career and finances.

It is important to point out that balance does not mean applying equal resources to every area of life. People sometimes imply this when they talk about work-life balance, as though they have divided their resources evenly between work and the rest of their life. That's not what we're talking about.

We fool ourselves if we think balance means giving equal attention to everything in our lives. Balance only happens in dynamic tension. Balance is giving not *equal* but *appropriate* attention to each of the various categories of your life. This will necessarily mean that some categories get more time and some less, but each will get the attention and resources necessary to keep it moving toward an intentional outcome.

And now as a guy who has led teams for the past thirty years and spent the last twenty coaching some of the busiest and most successful leaders in business, I know that how we lead ourselves in life impacts how we lead those around us. Self-leadership always precedes team leadership. We must have a balanced approach to accumulating net worth in all of the critical accounts in our lives, not just one or two. Ultimately this allows us to make the greatest difference and adds the most value to those around us. It is possible to grow at work without diminishing other areas of our lives. Living forward helps us find and maintain our balance.

Benefit No. 3: Filtering Opportunities

When starting out in your adult life, you scramble for opportunities. *If only I could get hired to work for this company or that organization*, you think. Or if you have a job, *If only I could get invited to work on this project or that one*. Initially, the opportunities may seem few and far between.

But as you progress through life—and if you are good at what you do—opportunities multiply. You get asked to take on more projects at work than you can manage. Your opportunities outside of work multiply too—social activities, volunteer projects, civic duties, and so on. There are so many really good opportunities in which you can invest your time.

Then there's your family. You want to invest time with your spouse and she wants time with you. It's not an unrealistic expectation, and you know it's important for your marriage. Then there's the growing honey-do list. Every time you fix or replace something, two new items get added to the list. And if you have children? The opportunities and activities multiply exponentially. Your kids are as busy as you are. Before you know it, you feel like a taxi driver, shuttling your kids between school, soccer practice, piano lessons, and birthday parties.

How did this happen so quickly? You are now flooded with opportunities and no clear way to decide when to say yes and when to decline. A Life Plan will enable you to filter your opportunities and focus on what matters most.

The year before I (Michael) wrote my first Life Plan, things were crazy. Work pressures were massive. Meanwhile, at home, there were Gail and our five daughters, ages twelve through twenty-two. They attended four different schools. Two were in college, two were in high school, and one was in middle school. In addition, the ones at home were active in soccer, basketball, guitar lessons, and the usual school projects. If you're wondering what the moments before a train wreck look like, I'm pretty sure that's it!

But once I had a Life Plan in place, it gave me the filter I needed to reprioritize and reorganize my life and start scaling back my activities. Things didn't change overnight, but I suddenly had the clarity—which gave me the courage—to manage my opportunities rather than be managed by them. I was finally able to say yes to what truly mattered and no to (almost) everything else.

Benefit No. 4: Facing Reality

In 1991 my business partner and I (Michael) suffered a financial meltdown. We had built a successful independent publishing company, but our growth outstripped our working capital. For a while our book distributor bridged the gap with cash advances on our sales. But soon their parent company wanted those advances back. Although we didn't officially go bankrupt, the distributor essentially foreclosed on us and took over all our assets.

It was a tough time. Confused, frustrated, and angry, I initially blamed the distributor. *If they had only sold more, as they had promised us, none of this would have happened. It's their fault.* But eventually I realized I was stuck until I took responsibility and learned what I could from the experience. Though incredibly difficult and humbling, the period taught me some critical, life-changing lessons that have brought me to where I am today.

You can't get where you want to go unless you start with where you are. Unfortunately, modern life seems to provide an endless array of distractions to avoid the difficult things of life. Worse, so much of pop culture tells us that our circumstances are someone else's fault.

The truth is, you can't improve what you won't face and own. The problems you encounter in your health, marriage, parenting, career, or personal finances will not just magically disappear. They have to be confronted and dealt with. This is difficult to do without outside help or a process that forces it.

Creating a Life Plan equips you to identify and address your current realities—not so you can beat yourself up, but so you can develop a plan for changing them and have the life you want.

Benefit No. 5: Envisioning the Future

Ron and Barb had been married for twelve years. They didn't have a bad marriage; it just wasn't great. They had settled into a comfortable level of coexistence. Ron pretty much did his thing. Barb pretty much did hers.

Feeling stuck in his life, Ron joined a mentoring group. The leader introduced the Life Planning concept and for the first time Ron acknowledged that his marriage had gone flat. More importantly, it gave him the opportunity to envision a different future. *What kind of relationship do I want with my wife?* Ron asked. *What might be possible?* The Life Planning process created a gap or felt need for Ron— something necessary for growth. Instead of settling for the status quo, he's now stretching toward a better future in his marriage.

Keeping your eye on the future is essential for making the most of today. You need to acknowledge where you are, but you also need to see clearly where you are going. What do you want in each of the major categories of your life? What would they look like in their ideal state?

A few years ago some clients sent my wife and me (Daniel) to the Maldives—a bucket list location for every surfer. While there, I worked with two surf coaches who photographed me in action. In some of the pictures I was sloppy and powerless. In others my form was much better. The difference all came down to where I was looking. Even though I had been surfing thirty years, the photos revealed a rookie mistake: when I took my eyes off the target, my form suffered. Where your eyes go, your body follows. Most beginners look at their feet—and they go down.

The lesson is simple. You get what you focus on. What we see ahead impacts the actions we take right now. How we live and lead is directly connected to what we see. What's important is that the future be enticing enough to stay focused. We call this *pull power.*

A goal needs to draw you. When I look into the future, I see that my wife, Sheri, and I at the age seventy-five are still each other's best and most intimate friends, and there is nobody we would rather spend time with than each other. We're still fueled by each other, we still play, and we enjoy life together. Pull power is essential to reach our goals. You need to see a future with such clarity and desirability that you will go through all the uncomfortable things life throws at you to attain it.

A Life Plan will equip you to envision a better, more compelling future. It provides an opportunity to use your imagination to create a better future. It then shows us where we have gaps so we can create plans and habits that will propel us forward. So many of us have settled for what is, rather than what could be. We have convinced ourselves that things will never change. But they can change if we give ourselves permission to dream again. What kind of future motivates you?

Benefit No. 6: Avoiding Regrets

Finally, a Life Plan will help ensure that you don't finish life with regrets. So many people get off track so easily. This is the problem with drift. And it's the problem with not being intentional.

A few years ago a friend had an affair. He didn't get up one morning and say, "You know, I think I'll have an affair today." No, it was more incremental and insidious than that. The drift pulled him under, and when he came up for air, his life was in shambles. His wife divorced him. His adult children refused to speak to him. And one by one, many of his friends walked off.

The worst part was that it seemed as if he refused to accept responsibility for his actions. He blamed his bad choices on others. He developed an entire narrative around it: His wife didn't provide him with the attention he needed. His career was boring, and he needed a diversion. His religious upbringing was legalistic and judgmental, almost forcing him to rebel. He couldn't help himself. Sadly, the drift and his inability or unwillingness to swim against the current took him places he never imagined going at the outset.

But it's not just the big tragedies we have to guard against. One of our clients, Garrett, wanted to become senior executive at his company, but there was a problem. The culture stank. He thought he could stay and affect the environment but soon realized it was making him miserable and spilling over into his other areas of life. He knew family was too important to allow that to continue, so he left. No regrets. In a moment of decision, his Life Plan kept him grounded. Garrett's family mattered, not fixing someone else's company. But what would have happened if he lost sight of that? There would have been plenty of regrets as his relationships suffered.

For many people, life has not turned out like they had hoped. They are disappointed, confused, and discouraged. But it doesn't have to be this way. While you can't control everything, you can control more than you think, and you can live your life with a plan that will dramatically improve your chances of ending up at a destination you choose. You can end up with no regrets. A Life Plan provides the insurance you need for success.

When You Lose Your Why

People lose their way when they lose their why. The reasons for creating a Life Plan are as varied as there are people. But the important thing is to connect with *your* reasons. What are the benefits you see to creating a Life Plan?

The more clear you can be about this at the outset, the more likely you will be to follow through and create your plan. More importantly, the more likely you will be to actually live it. And that, after all, is the real goal. In the next section, we'll show you exactly how to get started.

Part Two

CREATE YOUR PLAN

4

Design Your Legacy

All external expectations, all pride, all fear of embarrassment
or failure—these things just fall away in the face of death,
leaving only what is truly important.

—Steve Jobs

My (Daniel's) friend Mike was physically fit and about as
funny as he was smart. He played more practical jokes than
anyone I knew. Not even cancer could rob him of his sense
of humor.

The disease surprised everyone. Long into his battle, we
were having lunch. Mike talked about how cancer had height-
ened his awareness of the clock. He said he wished he could
have spent more time with the people who mattered most in
his life, starting with his dear wife, Gabby. "We all die," he
said. "I just did not fully realize it before." He felt like he'd
wasted a lot of time.

A few months later Gabby called me. Despite the treatments, the cancer had spread to Mike's brain. I flew out the next day to be with Mike in the hospital—the day after his thirty-eighth birthday.

I walked into the hospital room unannounced. There sat Mike in his bed, entangled in a web of wires and tubes. He was a shadow of his former self—emaciated by the cancer that racked his body. His eyes opened wide. "What are you doing here? Are you here for business, to surf . . . or what?"

"I'm just here to hang with you," I said. It was the first time I'd ever seen my strong friend scared. I could see it in his eyes and trembling hands.

Walking toward the bed, I asked Mike how he was doing. He grabbed my hand and answered, choking back the tears, "Not good. This is my worst nightmare, it is in my brain and I am not ready."

The two of us prayed. We talked about our families, our work, and the things that mattered most. Mike was not angry or filled with self-pity, just conflicted—trying to be brave, but struggling with the uncertainty of how the future would unfold and the fears that went along with that.

A few hours later I said my goodbyes, fighting back tears. "Don't feel sorry for me," Mike said, "I could outlive you. None of us know when we will go"—an unexpected and sobering truth if ever there was one.

Two hours later I boarded a plane for home. As I took off and flew above the California coastline, I took in a spectacular sunset over the Pacific and recalled seeing the sunrise that morning. Before that day I had always looked at a great sunrise or sunset as separate events. But my day with Mike and his passing, which happened not long after, reminded me that the setting is part of the rising.

The question for us is what happens in between. It's true for a day, and it's true for an entire life. The problem is that most of us are so caught up in our moment-to-moment activities, we don't stop to ask ourselves, *Where is this all going? How is it going to end if I stick to this same path?*

Play the movie of your life forward and find out. How? Keep reading.

Begin at the End

As we think about our legacy, we need to start with the end. This is obvious for other activities. The first thing you do in planning the family vacation, for example, is choose a destination. That determines everything else—the transportation required to get there, the clothing you will need to take with you, the accommodation options available, and the activities you might enjoy during your stay.

If it's true for enjoying a getaway, it's infinitely more so when it comes to mapping your life. What outcomes do you want? The end determines everything else—the characters you include in your story, the role they play in your life (and you in theirs), the projects you initiate, and the way you conduct your affairs.

There is a great Hebrew scripture that says, "Teach us to number our days, that we may gain a heart of wisdom."[1] Unless we take the time to regain our perspective and face the reality that life is short, we risk arriving at a destination we didn't choose—or at least one we wouldn't prefer.

For the past twenty years, Building Champions coaches have been directing our clients to write out their eulogy as if it were being read today. It is a powerful exercise that helps people prepare for the process of creating a meaningful and powerful Life Plan. Why? It engages both the head and the heart, which we have found to be critical for one's Life Plan to effect real and lasting change.[2] During your funeral, someone from your family—perhaps even a few friends—will offer a eulogy, a "good word" about your life. At the reception after the service, the words will continue. People will tell stories about you and express to one another what you truly meant to them. Imagine you could attend your own funeral and listen in to those conversations.

- What would those closest to you remember about your life?
- What stories would they tell one another?
- Would those stories make them laugh, cry, sigh, or all three?
- How would they summarize what your life meant to them?

Our days add up to a lifetime. At the end of that life, what will those closest to you say, what will they remember, how will they assess your legacy? The bad news is that once you're gone, you won't have any control over it. You will have passed on whatever you had—the good, the bad, or the ugly.

The good news is there's still time. The future is full of possibilities. You can still influence the conversations that will happen once you are gone. You can shape them by the choices you make from this point forward.

As we said in chapter 2, "Understand the Mission," a Life Plan is the answer to three powerful questions. It is time to answer question 1: *How do you want to be remembered?* This question forces you to consider your legacy.

Yes, You Will Leave a Legacy

Typically, we only use the word *legacy* when we talk about the rich and famous. Obviously, Abraham Lincoln left a legacy. So did Cornelius Vanderbilt. And Martin Luther King Jr. and Margaret Thatcher. But the rest of us? Absolutely.

Our legacy comprises the spiritual, intellectual, relational, vocational, and social capital we pass on. It's the sum total of the beliefs you embrace, the values you live by, the love you express, and the service you render to others. It's the you-shaped stamp you leave when you go.

Truth is, everyone is in the process of creating—and leaving—a legacy. The question is not "Will you leave a legacy?" but "What kind of legacy will you leave?" The sooner you come to grips with this reality, the sooner you can start creating it. Like it or not, your life now shapes your legacy then. You have an impact on everyone around you. You will influence the course of other people's lives for good or for bad. In other words, *your life matters*. You are here for a reason. Your job is to determine why.

The good news is that you can shape the memories of the people who matter most to you. The thoughts, words, and actions you choose will have an impact. We'll choose those in subsequent chapters, but here we want to help you clarify the memories you want to create.

As we suggest, it is helpful to visualize your own funeral. Ask, "How do I want to be remembered when I am gone?" What do you want the people closest to you to say?

Don't miss this step. The most compelling and effective Life Plans are created by those who are fully committed to the process of creating and following their plan. Every bit of you must go into this process. Be open and vulnerable with yourself. You want to capture your true values. By numbering your days and facing your mortality, you can engage your mind and heart in a compelling and powerful way.

"I feel like it has made me such a better leader," Janet told us when we asked her about the impact of Life Planning. "I am so much more compassionate and connected." She said this funeral exercise was the most eye-opening part of the process. It has helped her become more humble and self-aware, which has radically altered the culture of her business.

Writing Your Eulogy

One way to write a compelling eulogy is to create a series of short Legacy Statements that describe how you want to be remembered by the important people in your life. Here's how to do it.

1. *Identify your key relationships.* The first step is to identify the various groups of people who will attend your funeral. For the sake of this exercise, assume that everyone who is alive and in your life today, even if they are older than you, will be there. This includes family, friends, and work associates. We're not suggesting you write a paragraph about each person you expect at your funeral, because that could be many dozens or even hundreds of individuals. For example, "Work Associates" will suffice, without naming each person. The same is true of family members. "Children" covers the bases, without listing every one. Here are some possibilities of those who might attend your service:

- God
- Spouse

- Children and/or stepchildren
- Parents
- Siblings
- Colleagues
- Clients and teammates
- Friends
- Those you have mentored
- Community/church/synagogue members

Your list doesn't have to include all of these, by any means. And you'll want to personalize it. Use your husband's or wife's real name, for instance. The number of people or groups you include and the length of the Legacy Statement is totally up to you. The goal is to include as many and to write as much as you need to get a clear sense of how you'd like a broad spectrum of people to remember you. Keep in mind that these are just *possibilities*. The important thing is that these are people who represent the groups you can still influence. As long as they are alive and you are alive, you can have a positive impact.

2. *Describe how you want to be remembered by each group.* One way to do this is to use this sentence format: "I want [name or category of relationship account] to remember . . ." For example, this is how Karen, a stay-at-home mom, said she wants her husband to remember her:

I want Gary to remember that he was always my very best friend. I want him to remember how much he trusted me and how I always supported, valued, and encouraged his dreams and aspirations. I want him to remember what a powerful partnership we had and how our individual talents complemented our incredible marriage. I want him to remember how absolutely attracted we were to each other physically, mentally, and emotionally and how we always worked to fulfill each other's needs.

Here's how Chad, a high school history teacher, said he wants his children to remember him:

> I want to be remembered as a father who was deeply involved in their lives. I want them to think of how I would be able to talk about anything. I want them to remember how I was intentional in leading our family. I want them to remember how I would teach them through memorable experiences. I want to be known by the focused attention I gave to them.

Donna, a divisional executive for a large manufacturing company, said this is how she wants her colleagues at work to remember her:

> I want them to remember me as someone who served them and sought to develop them as leaders by setting aside my personal interests to help them achieve their personal and professional goals. I want them to affirm that I always told them the truth, even if the truth was difficult to hear, because they knew I loved them and wanted to serve them.

Finally, Eric, an online marketer, said this is how he wants his social media followers to remember him:

> I want them to remember my transparency, authenticity, and generosity. I want them to remember how I exceeded their expectations and gave them compelling, life-changing content and resources. Most of all, I want them to see in me a role model with a life worth emulating.

3. *Make your Legacy Statements as compelling as you can.* Remember, if your Life Plan will be compelling enough to shape your future, it must engage your mind *and* your heart.

Both are essential. One way to do the latter is to make your Legacy Statements as specific and concrete as possible. For example, rather than saying,

I want Sheila to remember the times we spent together.

you might instead say something like

I want Sheila to remember times we laughed, times we cried, times we spent discussing things that were important to both of us, and times we just held one another and watched the sunset.

These examples reflect how individuals want others to remember them. They all start with "I want so-and-so to remember . . ." and this is a great way to go. But if you have trouble getting started, you can try another tactic. Imagine your funeral as a scene in a movie. When family and friends stand to speak, what are they saying? Go ahead—you're writing the script. What do you want and hope they'll say? Capture those thoughts and you're well on your way.

When you are done, you should have a collection of Legacy Statements you can now form into your eulogy. The key is to write it as if your funeral were today, not a future date. Here's an example from Tom. You can see his and other examples of eulogies in the Life Plan examples in the back of the book:

Tom was known as a family man whose mission in life was to positively impact the lives of children. He and his wife, Lisa, made their children, grandchildren, and great-grandchildren priorities in their lives. Lisa was the love of his life, and they spent many days together in love and laughter, both as a couple and with their amazing family.

Tom's three children had him wrapped around their respective fingers from the day they were born. He coached many of their basketball and baseball teams when they were younger, always emphasizing the same lessons: have fun, hustle, and display good sportsmanship. His kids never forgot those lessons and realized they were applicable not only in sports but in life: have fun, work hard, and treat others with kindness and respect. After a lengthy career in the mortgage industry—including twenty years as the owner of a thriving mortgage company—Tom became a successful high-school basketball coach. Hundreds of the players he coached were in attendance at his memorial service, primarily because he cared more about them as people than as athletes.

The term *life balance* is one that Tom believed in wholeheartedly. He strived to instill the importance of balance into everyone he met, and his life was an example for others to follow.

By writing the eulogy as if it's being delivered today, you can begin thinking of what it will take to make those imagined memories real.

Make the Most of the Time Left

Eugene O'Kelly, former CEO of KPMG, one of the largest accounting firms in the world, was diagnosed with late-stage brain cancer at age fifty-three. His doctors soberly told him he had about three months to live. He quickly came to the conclusion that recovery was impossible. A miracle was unlikely. He was forced to do what most of us put out of our minds—think about his own impending death and the impact he had on others.

Over the next ninety days he determined he would die well. In true CEO fashion he created goals for himself. He made a list of important relationships he wanted to "unwind." By this he meant he wanted to bring closure to those relationships and communicate how much each person meant to him. Unlike us, he didn't have time to procrastinate. He couldn't just add this to his "someday/maybe" list, because he was out of days. Death was upon him.

During these last few months he decided he would create as many "perfect moments" as he could. His aim was to orchestrate experiences with others when time stands still—a time full of the present, when the past is left behind and the future is set aside.[3]

He consciously excluded interruptions and distractions. He turned his cell phone off. His heart was wide open. All that mattered for him was *this moment*—the people he was with and the conversation they were having *now*.

Even though his life was short, he made a lasting impact on those around him by becoming intentional with his remaining time. None of us know how long we have left. Do we have another thirty years—or thirty minutes? The parting statement of Mike, Daniel's friend, was spot on. We don't know. But we can make a difference and begin to shape our legacy now.

5

Determine Your Priorities

Decide what you want, decide what you are willing to exchange for it. Establish your priorities and go to work.

—H. L. Hunt

As the Great Recession began in August 2007, many of our clients were forced to radically cut spending. I (Daniel) was really feeling the pressure from a rapid loss of clientele. This was the beginning of a near-death experience for our company. My business partner, Barry, and I decided to take a day away from the turmoil and see if we could get some clarity. We took our fly rods and journals to the Deschutes River. Barry went upstream, I went down.

We met up several hours later. "What thoughts came to you?" Barry asked. I told him that I felt we were in the early stages of a very challenging season. My days were consumed with activities focused on keeping us afloat. Rather than being strategic with my time and priorities, I was being reactive and running from fire to fire. During my reflection time, I felt led to pull away from the business to gain some perspective and think of ways to innovate.

This was extremely counterintuitive for me, but it felt like the right thing to do. Plus, I knew my teammates would be able to handle the business without me for a bit (a great goal for any leader). As I headed out, I told Barry to call me only if the company somehow ran out of cash, which was a real possibility. The edge of the cliff wasn't far off.

I spent a few weeks with my family in Mexico and then two weeks with just my wife as we celebrated our twentieth anniversary. While I loved my business, my Life Plan reminded me of what was truly important. This time away was a rich, healthy time for me and my family. It was also an amazing thing for my business.

It was during this sabbatical that I crafted the content for a new product that saved the company's bacon—the Building Champions Experience. In addition to one-on-one coaching, it pushed the company into the conference space; reversed our losses; allowed us to serve clients in a fresh, new way in the middle of tough economic times; and positioned us to be a leader in the executive coaching industry. In the midst of economic trials that came in 2008, I doubt I would have been able to devote the necessary attention required to create and launch this huge new offering without the space that came from that sabbatical.

We tend to think effective people are busy. Not so, unless they're busy with the right things—and many people aren't. When things in our business or life get busy and hectic, we often lose sight of our priorities. But by keeping the truly important things front and center, we often get the perspective we need to make better decisions.

The people who live and lead with the most joy and contentment are those who have clarity about their priorities. They know what they do best and fill their days with more of those activities. If you can delegate, delay, or drop it, it may not be a priority for you. Or it shouldn't be.

We're not saying that if you figure out your priorities, your life will be utopian. But you might as well stack the odds in your favor, right? You have a limited supply of days. The wisest among us understand there are just fifty-two Saturdays in a year to be present with their kids. Are there other things to do on a Saturday? Of course. But if you don't figure out how to say no to good, you won't get to say yes to the great.

As we said earlier, a Life Plan is the answer to three powerful questions. Now it's time to answer question 2: *What matters most?*

What's Best for You?

This may be a question you have never considered. Perhaps you have let others decide what should be important—perhaps your parents, your spouse, or even your boss. We all face tremendous pressure in this regard.

External expectations about who we are and what we should do have a way of co-opting our value system. Many are told, for instance, they should go to college and perhaps even pursue an advanced degree. But why? Have you seen the statistics on jobless graduates? News outlets regularly run stories on the problem. It's practically a whole new genre of journalism—the indebted-graduate-who-can-explain-*Ulysses*-while-ringing-up-your-latte feature. Of course, there's nothing wrong with being a barista—as long as you want to be one or can afford to pay your college loan from the tip jar.

The reality is that despite the intense social pressure, college isn't for everyone. In their book *Is College Worth It?* former United States Secretary of Education William J. Bennett and liberal arts graduate David Wilezol rate the lifetime return on investment for several major colleges and universities. It turns out that high-performing high-school seniors would actually lose potential earning power if they went to certain colleges rather than go straight into the workforce after graduation.[1]

You have to do what's right for you. There is no point keeping up with the Joneses if they're going someplace you don't want to go. But you have to choose where you want to go before you can avoid the cultural drift. In this chapter, we want you to determine what's most important to you. What's essential? What are your priorities?

Identify Your Life Accounts

Start by thinking of all the various compartments that make up your life. Most people can organize their lives into seven to twelve distinct areas. We call these Life Accounts. Over the many years of coaching, here are the nine most common:

Note that the Life Accounts diagram is made up of three concentric circles emanating from the center—you.

The Circle of Being. The innermost ring is a collection of activities focused solely on you in relation to yourself. It includes your spiritual, intellectual, and physical accounts.

The Circle of Relating. The second ring is a collection of activities centered on you in relation to others: your marital,

FIGURE 5.1

NINE BASIC LIFE ACCOUNTS

parental, and social accounts (e.g., friendships, church or synagogue, book club, and so on).

The Circle of Doing. The third ring is a collection of activities dealing with you in relation to your output: your vocation (job), avocation (hobbies), and financial accounts.

This diagram is not a fixed or rigid model. It's just a way to help you recognize that your life is more than just one account. It is more than work. It is more than marriage. It is more than money. It is an interrelated collection of interests, responsibilities, dreams, and activities.

Your job in this section of the Life Plan is to create your own "Chart of Accounts." You want to write down a list of Life Accounts that are important to you.

We suggest you start with the nine depicted in the preceding diagram, but you are free to add and delete as you see fit. This is about your priorities, not ours. Your Chart of Accounts can have as many accounts as you want. We have seen Life Plans with as few as five accounts and as many as twelve.

For example, Jerry has nine:

- Self
- Marriage: Sandra
- Kids: Micah, Jeffery, and Annie
- Parents and Siblings
- Friends
- Career
- Finances
- Creating
- Pets

Hannah has eight:

- Faith
- Self-care
- Family: Charles, Julie, and Tommy
- Extended Family
- Finances
- Work
- Teaching
- Adventure

As you think through your own list, here are four considerations:

1. *Your Life Accounts are unique to you.* If you are currently single, you might not have a marital account. If you are newly married, you might not have a parental account. You also may not be at the stage of life where you want to add an avocational account (an area of interest or hobby you pursue outside your main occupation).

2. *Your Life Accounts can be named whatever you want.* Choose whatever name is meaningful to you, though we find it's best to apply specific names to the accounts when applicable. You can also choose an account that is broad in scope (e.g., a single account for your entire family) or narrower in scope (e.g., accounts for each member of your family—which can be really helpful because everyone has different needs). Again, it all depends on what is important to you and how narrowly you want to focus. The only thing we would caution you against is developing a list of more than ten to twelve accounts. In our experience, the individual accounts lose their meaning when there are too many.

3. *Your Life Accounts are interrelated.* For the purpose of discussion, we are asking you to list them separately. But this is only a model, not reality. In reality, you exist as a whole being with a whole life. If, for example, your health is poor, it could negatively influence your marriage, your work, and possibly even your spiritual life. Try as we might, we can't isolate the influence of one area from the others. Still, we want to list them, so we can give the appropriate amount of attention to each.

4. *Your Life Accounts will change over time.* We have updated our Life Accounts regularly over the years. How

we prioritize them changes too. (We'll have more to say about this in the next two sections.) The important thing is to develop a list that reflects your life *now*. Remember, as we said in chapter 2, your Life Plan is "a living document that you will tweak and adjust as necessary for the rest of your life."

Once you have your list of Life Accounts, it's time to evaluate how you fare in each.

Determine the Condition of Each

We can't improve what we don't assess, so this is a time to review each account and determine where you are. We have a tool for doing this that we will share with you in a moment. But first we want to explain why we chose the term *Life Accounts*.

Everyone understands how bank accounts work. They are a place to deposit your money, pay your bills, and accrue value. Moreover, each one has a specific balance:

Some accounts have a growing balance. You have more than you need. You are spending less than you take in. The balance is increasing. If most of your accounts are in this condition, your future is secure.

Some accounts have a consistent balance. You have what you need. You are spending about what you take in. The balance is holding steady. If most of your accounts are in this condition, your present may be secure, but your future may be in jeopardy.

Some accounts have a declining balance. You have less than you need. You are spending more than you take in.

76

The balance may be overdrawn. If you have too many accounts in this condition, neither your present nor your future is secure. You risk going "bankrupt."

Now, take this financial metaphor and apply it to your Life Accounts. Each has a specific balance. Some are growing, some are holding steady, some are declining or are overdrawn. For example, you're killing it in your soccer league, but your family misses you on weekends. Or maybe you're beating your goals at work, but your health account is overdrawn—you're eating too much junk food and you are not exercising regularly. Or perhaps you're in great shape physically, but your marriage has gone flat—you and your spouse have become like strangers living in the same house. Or maybe you have lost your job, but you have a wonderful circle of friends who stand with you.

The point is, your life is a collection of accounts and each of them requires the right attention. In this section, we provide a tool for helping you assess the condition of each Life Account so you can give it the attention it needs to accomplish your overall objectives.

The Life Assessment Profile is an online tool designed to help you determine if each of your Life Accounts is getting what it needs. You can find it at LivingForwardBook.com.

This online assessment takes approximately twenty minutes to complete. When you finish, we email you a three-page report that shows you exactly where you stand in each of your Life Accounts. This will serve as the foundation for creating your Action Plans in chapter 6.

The conceptual model for the Life Assessment Profile looks like this:

FIGURE 5.2

THE LIFE ASSESSMENT PROFILE ™

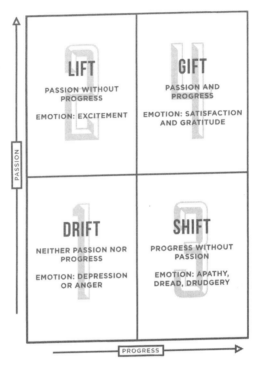

The goal is to have a positive balance in each of your Life Accounts. But what exactly does that mean? In our experience, people have a positive account balance when they experience both *passion* and *progress*. These are two distinct but essential components.

Passion relates to your enthusiasm for a specific Life Account. Are you in love with your spouse? Is that love growing or waning? What about your career? Are you passionate about your work or are you bored with it? Or what about your health? Do you love to exercise or do you hate it? Regardless, this is what we mean when we talk about passion.

Progress relates to the results you are getting in a specific Life Account. Again, what about your spouse? You might love him or her but you constantly fight. What about your career? You might love your work, but don't make what you think you deserve or haven't been promoted to the level you want. Or what about your health? You enjoy exercise but are still heavier than you'd like.

To illustrate how passion and progress play out in real life, consider the situation in which I (Michael) found myself after a very successful career in book publishing. I got into the business because I loved books. I was fascinated by the potential they had for changing the world. I also enjoyed working with authors, helping them give birth to their ideas.

But as I moved up the corporate ladder, I found myself working less and less with authors and more and more in corporate administration and financial oversight. I was good at it and got promoted every twelve to eighteen months— eventually making president and CEO. But the fact that the company published books was almost immaterial at that point. My job was mostly about keeping the board happy by growing revenues and cutting costs.

And I hated it. I had certainly seen progress but had lost the passion.

We see these kinds of real-world examples all around us.

- The waiter who loves singing and playing the guitar (*he has the passion*) but can't get a gig that pays enough to meet his needs (*he is not seeing progress*).
- The mom who loves her children and wants to be successful as a parent (*she has the passion*) but whose children are disrespectful and out of control (*she is not seeing progress*).

- The dentist whose practice is growing steadily (*he is seeing progress*) but hates the monotony of working on people's teeth day after day (*he has lost his passion*).
- The couple who has an efficient relationship—a clear understanding of their respective roles and responsibilities (*they have seen progress*)—but they just don't enjoy one another's company like they used to (*they have lost their passion*).

Again, the Life Assessment Profile™ measures passion and progress in each of your major Life Accounts. This is not a scientific instrument—but it is a helpful construct for you to evaluate how you are doing in each of the areas that you have determined are important to you.

Based on your passion and progress scores, the profile will plot where you are on a two-by-two matrix or grid as shown earlier in figure 5.2. For each Life Account, you will be in one of four states:

Drift. This is the state of no passion and no progress. It is the worst possible state you can be in with one of your Life Accounts. If you fall here, you probably experience some disappointment, anger, apathy, or perhaps despair. To escape this negative spiral, something must change. You need to rekindle your passion and figure out how to get positive results. By the way, passion usually precedes progress because it's the natural driver for progress.

Lift. This is the state of having passion but not experiencing progress. The fact that you are passionate is good, but it is not enough. You are probably excited, but if you don't begin to see results, this can quickly turn to disappointment or, worse, cynicism. You need to focus on implementing a new strategy, acquiring new skills, or doing something that sparks the progress you want.

Shift. This is the state of experiencing progress without passion. You are moving forward, but you don't really care. You are not enjoying this area of your life. Maybe you are feeling apathy, dread, or a sense of drudgery. Your heart isn't in it. You need to focus on rekindling your passion, becoming fascinated with something you haven't noticed before, or somehow connecting with the importance of this area.

Gift. This is the state of experiencing both passion and progress. It is the best possible state you can be in with one of your Life Accounts. If you are in this state, you likely feel satisfied and grateful. You hope it never ends. You need to figure out how you got here, so you can keep doing it and even take it to a new level.

The purpose of completing the Life Assessment Profile™ is to give you the benchmarks you need to move from where you are to where you want to be in every area of your life. We will use this information when we get to chapter 6, "Chart the Course."

But we still have one more step to take in answering the question, "What matters most to you?"

Prioritize Your Life Accounts

David worked for a global firm that wanted him to relocate to Hong Kong. It was a major step up, a huge promotion. But it came with costs. He would have had to leave his family for two years. Sure, he'd be able to return home every few weeks, and all the miles he'd rack up would mean it would be easy for his family to visit, but that couldn't erase the fact that twenty-six nights a month, Dad would be on another continent. If he were away that much, it doesn't take a genius to determine that his kids wouldn't care if he was around as they got older.

At the same time this offer came in, so did another. It was less glamorous, but good. He didn't have to move. But because he had no clarity on his priorities, Dave had a tough time deciding which position to take.

When faced with a choice like this in your life, what's the best answer? Start by fast-forwarding the movie of your life. What happens if you put the jet-set lifestyle ahead of your family needs? Dave saw the end of that movie and took the local job.

I, Daniel, had to do the same. At the height of my career in the mortgage business, I received a massive promotion. With it came extensive travel, and I was on planes two to three days each week coaching and developing all of our branch leaders throughout the western US. I was being groomed for the C-suite and had just turned thirty. From a career and income perspective, my future looked better than I could have ever imagined.

Then I realized I was chasing the wrong things. I had a beautiful bride and three young kids, and they needed me far more than my company did. I was clear on my priorities, but the time I was investing in each was out of order. I was on my way to real wealth in a few accounts and bankruptcy in others. My priorities were out of whack. Coming to this realization led to my first sabbatical. It lasted for one year and led to some of the most significant changes in my life. One of those was launching the coaching company that is responsible for the content of this book.

Having priorities is essential. So is having them in the right order. It's time to take your list of Life Accounts and arrange them in priority order from most important to least important. Obviously all of them are important, otherwise they wouldn't be on your list. But not all of them have the *same* importance.

For example, your career is important—but probably not more than your family. Yet, so many people live as though work is their highest priority. Ranking your Life Accounts forces you to decide what takes precedence if push comes to shove. And shoving will happen, guaranteed.

Place a number beside each Life Account, indicating its priority in relationship to the other accounts. For example, Heidi's prioritized list looks like this:

1. Jonah and Grace
2. Ian
3. My nephews
4. Brothers and sisters-in-law
5. Mom and Dad
6. Colleagues
7. Friends
8. Community
9. Extended Family

Greg's looks like this:

1. God
2. Myself
3. Terri
4. Alex and Michelle

5. My parents and siblings
6. Career/ministry
7. Friends
8. Finances

The order you choose is up to you. This is going to become the plan for your life. Ask, "What is the most important Life Account in my list? What is the one I would not be willing to sacrifice no matter what?"

The only Life Accounts we would recommend that you put near the top of your list are those related to yourself. For you, this might be a single account or three separate ones as we suggested (i.e., Spiritual, Intellectual, and Physical). Here's why: You can't take care of anyone else unless you first take care of yourself.

If you've traveled by plane, you've undoubtedly heard the flight attendant say something like this: "In the event of a change in cabin pressure, panels above your head will open revealing oxygen masks." If you've traveled more than occasionally, you can probably recite the rest of the spiel: "Pull the mask down toward you to activate the flow of oxygen. Cover your nose and mouth with the mask. Place the elastic band around your head and continue to breathe normally." And then they always say, "Remember to secure your own mask before assisting others."

Why? Because if you run out of air, you can't help anyone. Here is a little insight into how we look at life. We have to attend to ourselves first (second only to God for us) in order to be spiritually, emotionally, intellectually, and physically available to others.

If you have trouble with the semantics of putting yourself first, think of it as preparation to serve others. For example,

- If you aren't fed spiritually, you won't have the resources to edify others. This is why we strive to read the Bible and pray daily.
- If you don't look after your health and become sick, you can't best serve your family or co-workers. This is why we exercise regularly and eat nutritionally.
- If you don't make time for reading great books, you won't have the intellectual resources you could otherwise have to share with others. This is why we strive to read at least a book or two a month and listen to others audibly when exercising or traveling.
- If you don't make the effort to work through your emotional wounds, you end up reacting to others instead of being in a position to help them. This is why we take regular emotional audits and uproot any seed of bitterness we find growing.
- If you don't get sufficient rest, you get grumpy and nobody wants to be around you. This is why we try to sleep seven-plus hours nightly. Plus, we want to model how to take care of ourselves, so that those we lead will take care of themselves.

There will be seasons of self-sacrifice. Sadly, some people put themselves at the bottom of their priority list in every season. This is a bad idea, because you are in a much better position to serve others when your basic needs are met and your "tank is full."

Lots of Moving Parts

This chapter may lead you to think your life has a lot of moving parts. That's because it does! So often we delude ourselves into giving attention to one Life Account at the expense of the others. When this happens, it is only a matter of time before the other accounts become overdrawn. When you have too many of these happen at one time, you go bankrupt, figuratively speaking.

A list ranked in order of priority will ensure this doesn't happen for you. It doesn't mean that the balance on one of your accounts won't sink low or be overdrawn from time to time, but if the others have positive balances, you can handle it. And you define what account success looks like. In the next chapter, we'll learn to create Action Plans that ensure our account balances are positive and growing.

6

Chart the Course

"Would you tell me, please, which way I ought to go from here?"

"That depends a good deal on where you want to get to," said the Cat.

"I don't much care where—" said Alice.

"Then it doesn't matter which way you go," said the Cat.

—Lewis Carroll, *Alice in Wonderland*

For the past sixteen years or so, I (Daniel) have participated in Hood to Coast, the largest relay race in North America. Over a thousand teams run nonstop almost two hundred miles from Timberline Lodge, which sits at 6,000 feet on Oregon's majestic Mount Hood, down through several small cities, farmland, hillsides, Portland, and then over the coastal mountain range. The finish line is the Pacific—specifically, Seaside Beach—where about fifty thousand people gather to celebrate the achievement.

Hundreds of volunteers cover the course and you can download an app to stay on track. But when I first started running it in the late nineties, the volunteers were few and the apps nonexistent. Runners were given a map with mileage and major street markers. And that was about it.

Once, after looking at the map at 3:30 in the morning, I set out for my second of three runs. I had a pretty good idea of where I was supposed to go. The moon was out, I had a nice pace, and I was feeling great. Suddenly, three runners came up behind me and blew past our turn. I yelled, "Hey, you missed our turn!" They slowed down, and I recognized one from the Oregon State University track team a few years back. They told me they had the right course and convinced me to catch up and run with them.

You know how the story goes from here.

About fifteen minutes and two miles later, they started to have doubts. We slowed down and finally stopped to debate our direction. My panic and frustration rose, especially because I knew I'd let my team down. I could just see them at the exchange, worried when we failed to show on time—being more than thirty minutes late at an exchange usually means something bad happened.

Having clarity on where you want to go is one of the most critical components of your Life Plan. Knowing the course is critical to finishing the race well and on time. If we're not crystal clear where we're headed, we may allow other well-meaning people or exciting opportunities to influence us and then make decisions we later regret.

One of the core exercises we coach our clients through is to write a vision for their businesses that is both clear and compelling. When we have clarity on our destination and are grounded in our current reality, we are equipped to make the best decisions possible. We believe the same is true for our lives as well.

As we said in chapter 2, "Understand the Mission," a Life Plan is the answer to three powerful questions. We have answered the first two, so now it is time to answer question 3: *How can I get from here to where I want to be?* Put another way, how do I properly chart the course I'll take? We suggest breaking each Life Account down into five sections.

Section 1: Purpose Statement

In this section you state what your purpose is for each Life Account. How do you determine your purpose? Think of it this way. Imagine you were *assigned* this account. What would be your primary responsibility? What's your role? That is your purpose.

Jon, for example, wrote this in his Health Account:

My purpose is to maintain and care for the temple God has given me.

June wrote this in her Spouse Account:

My purpose is to be the love of Andy's life, his primary cheerleader, and his soul mate.

Stuart wrote this in his Friends Account:

My purpose is to befriend and love a few people well, who will in turn love, challenge, and hold me accountable.

Section 2: Envisioned Future

This is where you describe how the account looks when you have a "positive net worth." In a financial account it is easy to see. If the number is positive, it's good; if it's negative—or in the red—it's bad.

With Life Accounts you have to do a little more work. You want to describe the account when it's functioning at its best—as if it's already a *reality*. This is crucial. To help you capture your envisioned future, we suggest you take these steps:

Stand in the future. People are pretty talented at being somewhere, anywhere, besides where they are. We rehash the past and obsess about the future. This often feels like a curse. We struggle to live in the present. But let's put this tendency to time-travel to our advantage. Project yourself to a future time—maybe three years, ten years, any point you choose. The important thing is to picture yourself consciously at that future point. Are you there now? Good. Now stay there as you work through this process.

Make your imagination work for you. Most of us use our power to imagine the future the wrong way. We regularly envision a grim future full of worry. Instead, consciously visualize positive possibilities. If you can imagine a future, you can imagine a better one.

Employ all five senses. As you begin to envision the future, the more concrete you can be, the better. You need to see, hear, smell, taste, and feel it. The more you can do this, the more compelling it will be. Start by describing what you see. Some organizations do this by crafting short films to excite employees, consumers, and investors about what the future will look like as people use their products. Corning produced a series called "A Day Made of Glass" (LivingForwardBook.com/corning). And Microsoft created a series of its own called "Productivity Future Vision" (LivingForward

Book.com/microsoft). You may not be able to turn your vision statement into a short film, but you want to be so vividly clear in your sensual imagery that you could if you had the resources.

Record what you see. Writing our thoughts forces us to get clear about them. We won't kid you, this is hard work. It might be the most difficult part of creating a Life Plan. But it is vital to the process. You don't have to get it perfect, but you do have to get it down. Once you do, you can tweak and revise it over time. But it all begins when you start *writing*.

Use the present tense. To make your newly envisioned future as real and compelling as possible, describe it in the *present tense* as though you were standing in the midst of it.

For example, rather than saying:

> I want to be lean and strong, possessing vibrant health and extraordinary fitness.

Say:

> I am lean and strong, possessing vibrant health and extra-ordinary fitness.

Do you see the difference? Or, rather than saying:

> I will become debt-free. I want to have a six-month emergency fund. I want to achieve financial independence, so I could sustain my current lifestyle indefinitely—even without additional income. I hope to have all the money I need to meet my obligations and accomplish my goals.

Say:

> I am completely debt-free. I have a six-month emergency fund. Because I am financially independent, I could sustain

my current lifestyle indefinitely—even without additional income. I have all the money I need to meet my obligations and accomplish my goals.

The difference between each set of statements is subtle but central to what we're doing. Fantasizing about the future doesn't do much good by itself, but when presented with a clear and compelling picture, our minds get busy trying to make it a reality. We consciously try to close the distance between where we are and where we see ourselves, actively formulating plans and next actions. What's really important is that we believe we can achieve our goal. If we believe we can, even our subconscious gets to work, problem-solving and directing our focus. The more belief and confidence we feel toward achieving our goal, the higher the probability of our making the changes required to hit our targets.[1]

After following these five steps, I (Michael) wrote this down for my Health Account:

I am lean and strong, possessing vibrant health and extraordinary fitness. My heart is strong and healthy. My arteries are supple and clear of obstructions. My autoimmune system is in excellent condition; I am disease-, infection-, and allergy-resistant. I have more than enough energy to accomplish the tasks I undertake. This is because I control my mental focus, work out six days a week, choose healthy foods, take supplements as needed, and get adequate rest.

I (Daniel) wrote this for my Health Account:

At the age of 65 I am trim and fit, able to run the Hood to Coast, surf, and play with my grandkids. I have maximum energy and maintain this until I leave here.

Section 3: Inspiring Quote

Search for a quote that resonates with the core of your future purpose. This could be anything you find personally inspiring. It is optional, but some people find it very useful. It could be a verse, a proverb, a famous saying, any thought you find compelling.

Susan uses this adaptation of a quote from Lawrence Pearsall Jacks for her work account:

> The master in the art of living makes little distinction between his work and his play, his labor and his leisure, his mind and his body, his information and his recreation, his love and his religion. He hardly knows which is which. He simply pursues his vision of excellence at whatever he does, leaving others to decide whether he is working or playing. To him he's always doing both.[2]

John uses this Joyce Meyer line for his Health Account:

> I believe that the greatest gift you can give your family and the world is a healthy you.

I (Daniel) use a line from Proverbs for my Self-Improvement account:

> Make your ear attentive to wisdom, Incline your heart to understanding.[3]

There's no right or wrong way to do this. The important thing is to find something that inspires *you*.

Section 4. Current Reality

Now it's time to be honest with yourself. Where are you in relationship to your envisioned future? Don't pull any punches. The more honest you can be, the more progress you will see. But don't get discouraged. The whole point of a Life Plan is to move beyond your current circumstances.

We recommend that you keep it simple and list these as a series of bullets. Try to write down the first things that come to mind without too much analysis. For example, here's what I (Michael) wrote a while back in my Health Account:

- I feel great. My stamina is great. It's been a long time since I have been sick.
- I feel good about my weight and my overall fitness.
- I am running (or cross-training) four days a week for at least 60 minutes.
- I am not presently doing consistent strength training. I am concerned this will eventually catch up with me. (I know strength is particularly important as I age.)
- I am eating pretty well, but I could be more consistent in avoiding high glycemic carbs.

We would share more, but frankly it's too personal. Make yours very intimate too. It's not for public consumption. You want it to be so real and honest you would only share it with one or two people you've positioned in your life for the sake of accountability, perhaps including a coach.

Section 5. Specific Commitments

This is where you commit to specific actions to move from your current reality to your envisioned future. Again, we recommend these as a series of bullets.

While these aren't goals per se, they function like goals and should be SMART. The acronym is used a lot and is interpreted in different ways by different teachers. We suggest that your specific commitments meet these five criteria:

- Specific—your goals must identify exactly what you are committing to with as much specificity as you can muster. We're talking nonnegotiable disciplines you can schedule—so clear you can pull them from your plan and drop them right into your calendar.
- Measurable—as the adage says, "You can't manage what you can't measure." If possible, quantify the result. You want to know absolutely, positively whether or not you fulfilled your commitment.
- Actionable—make every commitment start with an action verb (e.g., "quit," "run," "finish," "eliminate," etc.) rather than a to-be verb (e.g., "am," "be," "have," etc.)
- Realistic—you have to be careful here. A good commitment should stretch you, but you need a dose of common sense.
- Time-bound—every commitment needs a time period associated with it. Unlike a goal, it doesn't necessarily need a due date, but you should note the frequency, if not explicitly, then implicitly.

I (Michael) made these specific commitments in my Health Account:

- Run (or cross-train) four days a week.
- Do strength training three days a week.
- Drink four liters of water a day.
- Make healthy food choices, as recommended in *The South Beach Diet*.

- Record daily everything I eat in MyFitnessPal (a software application that tracks your calorie intake and exercise output).
- Get an annual physical and semiannual dental checkup.

I (Daniel) wrote this in my account for Sheri:

- Pray with Sheri daily before going to sleep.
- Spend the last 30 minutes of each night communicating with her. Use this time to encourage, honor, respect, support, accept, and love her by giving eye-to-eye and ear-to-ear time with no interruptions.
- Date Sheri every week. A date can be for breakfast, lunch, or dinner during the week or a night out, but it is just the two of us. Monday afternoon date plus one date night per week.
- Take Sheri away for an overnight getaway monthly.
- Invite her to join me on my Sabbath days at the coast and organize care for the kids so she can join me.
- Help her to coordinate her getaway with Allie, Sheryl, and Talia.
- Plan for a special anniversary experience before June 1st.
- Pursue her heart through romance and intimacy daily.

To see what a complete Action Plan looks like, here are a couple of examples. Remember, these are directional, not dogmatic. We provide them so you can get a better idea about structuring your own.

This is one for Monica's Rest Account:

———— Action Plan ————

Account Name: Rest

Purpose Statement:

My purpose is to stay connected to my heart and my family by not letting my demanding career crowd out the things that matter most.

Envisioned Future:

I take the time I need to rest and recharge on nights, weekends, and vacations to ensure I can be my best for those who need me most. I feel in control of my schedule and restored each day by my personal and family time in the evenings. Ron and I take a long weekend away from the kids once a quarter, and we take the kids on a getaway for spring and fall break.

Inspiring Quote:

"Each of us needs to withdraw from the cares which will not withdraw from us."—Maya Angelou

Current Reality:

- I'm working too much in the evenings. I make time for the kids, but spend more time with my email than Ron.
- I'm only getting five to six hours sleep each night.
- I'm mostly successful not working Saturday and Sunday.
- I'm taking my lunch to the park, which gives me a chance to pause and recharge.
- Ron and I only made two of our quarterly getaways last year.

Specific Commitments:

- Limit evening email to fifteen minutes.
- Boost my nightly sleep to seven hours and stick to it!
- Keep taking lunch to the park, weather permitting.
- Plan biweekly date nights with Ron at least three months out.

- Schedule quarterly getaways with Ron a year in advance. Do it by October 15.
- Save 1 to 3 p.m. every Saturday for a nap.

Here is an Action Plan for Mark's Finances Account:

———— Action Plan ————

Account Name: Finances

Purpose Statement:
My purpose is to be a good steward of the financial resources at my disposal.

Envisioned Future:
Gretchen and I never worry about money. We follow a budget, with "blow money" for fun. We are debt-free and financially independent with all the resources necessary to cover our immediate obligations and accomplish our long-term goals. We have six months' worth of expenses in an emergency fund in case one of us loses our job. Having enough for ourselves, we give generously to our favorite charities.

Inspiring Quote:
"You must gain control over your money or the lack of it will forever control you." Dave Ramsey

Current Reality:
- The budget is set and we're following it.
- We give 10 percent of our income each month.
- Our monthly expenses suck every penny now except our giving and 401(k) contribution.
- We've saved two months' worth of expenses for emergencies.
- We need to buy a new car early next year and only have $6,800 saved so far.

Specific Commitments:

- Fatten the emergency fund with another month's worth of expenses by year's end.
- Cut at least $200 of monthly expenses and roll it into the emergency fund starting next month.
- Keep saving $250 monthly for car purchase.
- Keep meeting with Gretchen Sunday nights, 8 to 9 p.m., to review the budget and expenses.

Create an Action Plan like these for *each* of your Life Accounts.

Incremental Change

While our friend, author and executive coach Dr. Henry Cloud, was struggling through his doctoral dissertation, someone gave him an ant farm. It was a curious gift, but Cloud set it up. It didn't take his ants long before they were hauling grains of sand here and there in the glass terrarium.

Why they were doing it wasn't exactly clear, but it became clear when Cloud returned after a few days away. Suddenly he could see tunnels and structures taking shape. "It wasn't much longer," says Cloud, "and an entire ant city had been built." Each ant—by moving his solitary grain of sand at a time—built something truly impressive.[4]

It was the inspiration (and instruction) Cloud needed to finish his dissertation, and it's a lesson we can use too. When you are writing your Action Plans, it's easy to underestimate the power of incremental change. Some people think they must take massive action to achieve anything significant.

Sometimes big steps are necessary. We've certainly used them to achieve certain results. But if we make the job too daunting, we can get demotivated and give up before we ever start. Don't make that mistake! Maybe your challenge is finishing a dissertation like Cloud. Perhaps instead you've got a significant weight-loss goal, a substantial savings target, a need to improve your golf score, or a foreign language to learn. Whatever the goal, small, daily investments can bring big results. Just move the grain of sand a little each day.

Here are several examples to get your creativity flowing:

Losing weight. A few years ago, I (Michael) lost eleven pounds in six weeks. A friend lost more than eighty in a year. We both did it using LoseIt, a free iPhone app. We didn't do much besides record what we ate each day. By becoming aware of what we were eating, we made healthier choices. The cumulative power of those little daily decisions added up to—or rather, subtracted—a lot!

Health. I (Daniel) have a dear friend who is one of the top-ranked triathletes nationally in his age group of fifty and older. But he wasn't always in great shape. Seven years ago he'd never even run a marathon. I helped him with his first, and more races followed. By adjusting his daily schedule to include time to run, swim, or ride, he was eventually ready for the grueling Hawaiian Ironman. Incremental adjustment to his routine transformed him, his health, and even his marriage—his wife now competes with him.

Improving profitability. In a publishing division I (Michael) once ran, we decided to improve our margins by 2 percent in twelve months. We chunked it down to ½ percent per quarter. Taking it in bite-sized pieces enabled us to implement very practical measures. With targeted price increases and expense control, our team moved more than a million dollars to the bottom line that year.

Paying off debt. One of our friends wanted to pay off all of her personal debt. She didn't do anything radical. She simply established a budget, took opportunities to earn extra income, and cut back on gourmet coffee and other nonessentials. Using Dave Ramsey's "debt snowball" process, she paid off her smallest debts first, then the larger ones. In all, she knocked out $15,000 in less than twelve months.

Marriage. About a decade ago, Sheri and I (Daniel) had our fourth child. We'd been married fifteen years and our oldest was already a young teen. To say our lives were full during this season would be an understatement. Unfortunately, we were not as connected as we had been in earlier years. So we decided to start dating Mondays at lunch—a time to sync up, connect, talk about our week, our schedules, kids, and so on. By handling the life management stuff at lunch, we were free to enjoy much richer date nights. Nine years later, I credit the discipline of those regular, weekly lunch dates for the present-day health of my marriage.

We're convinced you can do almost anything if you are willing to clarify your commitments and make incremental investments over time to achieve them. Little daily decisions and course corrections are the story of our lives—that's why they matter. Action Plans help you intentionally leverage the power of incremental change.

7

Dedicate One Day

A plan in the heart of a man is like deep water, but a man
of understanding draws it out.[1]

—Solomon

Imagine we're standing along the edge of a lake next to an
SUV. The hatch is up and a large open chest sits in the back
of the vehicle. Go ahead, have a look. You can see that it's
stacked to the top with $100 bills. To save you the hassle of
counting, we'll just tell you—it's $3 million.

That much cash is heavy, of course, especially when you
throw in the weight of the watertight chest. Now that we've
secured the lid, we'll need your help getting it into the boat.

After thanking you for the assistance, we leave you at the
edge and row out to the middle of the lake. It's a ways out,
but you can see everything perfectly. We grab the chest on
either end, hoist it over the side, and—you can hardly believe

your eyes—drop it into the murky water below! A few minutes later and we're back on the shore. We leave the boat in your care, shake hands, hop into the SUV, and drive away.

Now what are you going to do?

Here's a good guess: You'll pull out your cell phone and try to find the nearest available dive shop, while you keep your eye exactly on the spot you saw us drop the money. It doesn't matter what you have planned. All appointments are canceled, meetings postponed, calls forgotten. Expense reports? To-dos? Your inbox? Forget about it. Your schedule just changed. If you know the location of $3 million, you'll drop everything to go find it.

If you take your eye off the spot, if you leave and come back, if you get distracted by whatever else is nearby, you may lose it. You may miss your shot. It's the same with Life Planning. At this point in the book, we have shared everything you need to know to create your Life Plan. But the longer you delay in seizing the treasure, the more likely you'll lose it. The time to act is now.

If you've heard renowned business and life thought leader Jim Rohn's "law of diminishing intent," you know why this is important. The law of diminishing intent says that the longer you delay doing something, the less probability you have of actually doing it. You lose all the emotional energy. That's why we encourage you to schedule a day within the next two weeks to create your Life Plan.

This is not something you can do piecemeal. In this chapter we explain why it's vital that you put everything else in your life on hold and set aside a full day. We cover the right approach and preparation for this important day as well, but the main thing to remember is that this is the day that can change everything for you.

Why a Full Day Is Important

The course of history has often turned on a single day. On July 4, 1776, fifty-six delegates to the Continental Congress approved the Declaration of Independence and changed world history. On June 6, 1944, Allied forces invaded Normandy and began the military push that liberated Europe. On August 28, 1963, under the visionary leadership of Martin Luther King Jr., more than 250,000 Americans marched on Washington, DC, paving the way for the Civil Rights Act of 1964.

One day can change everything. It's true for nations and individuals. Think back on your own graduation, wedding, or promotion. Or maybe things far less pleasant: a cancer diagnosis, the end of a marriage, or the death of a loved one. For better or worse, some days have more impact on the future than others.

This is particularly true of the day you create your first Life Plan. Done well, this singular event will affect not only your life but possibly the lives of generations that follow. You will unleash a set of decisions and actions that will have a greater impact than you could possibly imagine.

Despite the importance, some people balk at the thought of giving up an entire day for this exercise. They think, *Who has time for that?* Instead, they want to create their Life Plan incrementally, over a span of days or weeks. But after guiding thousands of people through this process, we can tell you this approach is ineffective. The best course is not a series of weekly appointments, or even two half days. It takes *one full day* to do it right.

Solomon said, "A plan in the heart of a man is like deep water, but a man of understanding draws it out." Like that chest in the lake, we have plans and desires deep in our hearts.

But the sad truth is that most people fail to coax them out and live from the wealth they afford. They get distracted, lose focus, and give up. Only the wise find the prize.

We've mentioned already the profound words of the Hebrew poet: "Teach us to number our days, that we may gain a heart of wisdom." You don't have an infinite supply of days to make a difference in the lives of your loved ones, family, and friends, and in the world. The wise know their days are numbered and act accordingly.

As we mentioned earlier, a Life Plan needs pull power. It has to be done in such a way that impacts your heart, not just your head. Otherwise, you'll just end up with a glorified to-do list. And who needs one more of those? Pull power requires that you get caught up in the full scope of the plan. You can't do that piecemeal. If you write out your epitaph between two and three on a Friday afternoon but then don't work on your Life Accounts till the following Thursday, you will have lost the emotional power of the previous exercise.

No, something this significant deserves an immersive experience. Life is full of distractions. Life Planning requires unplugging from the other demands on our attentions. Thinking about your life—your whole life—is different than solving the next problem on your daily task list. There's a certain amount of ramp-up time. It requires focused attention. You need a full day to get into the groove and really ponder where you have been and where you are going.

This is not merely an intellectual exercise. If you try to knock it out in a few hours, rather than give it the time it requires, you're short-circuiting the creative process. Life Planning is fundamentally about imagining a better future. It's about breaking free of your limiting beliefs, tapping into your deepest desires, and standing in the realm of possibility.

You need the time to work through each Life Account, see it in relationship to the whole, and imagine what can be.

Bottom line: This is the biggest day of your year. If you're going to assess every aspect of your life, it's worthy of your full attention. Total focus means greater impact. We are asking you to make a decision. Will you commit to taking a full day, 8 a.m. to 5 p.m., to work on your Life Plan? Yes or no?

Get Off Your But

People who resist the idea of committing to a full day usually cite one of the following five excuses. We thought we'd hit these head-on just in case they were about to slip out of your lips.

> *But I'm too busy.* This is an all-purpose excuse for people who just don't want to do something. You're busy. So is everybody else. We get it. But the truth is, people make time for what is important to them. The real question is whether or not you think Life Planning is important. The busier you are, the more intentional you must be. Otherwise, you amplify your risk of drifting to a destination you didn't choose.

> *But I can't afford to.* Maybe you work in a job where you don't get a vacation or paid time off. Committing a day to Life Planning means lost income or, at the very least, lost opportunity. You'd like to devote a full day to creating your plan, but it will cost you to do so. First of all, you don't have to do this on a workday. Any day you typically take off can provide a terrific time to do it. You might not have to take time off from work. But if you do, we encourage you to reframe this as an *investment*

rather than a cost. What could be a better use of your time than establishing a game plan for your life?

But I'm not a writer. A Life Plan isn't a novel. This document won't be published. In fact, you don't have to let *anyone* read it (though you might choose to share it with a close friend, coach, or someone who can help you live it out). This is purely for your own consumption. If you can think it, you can write it. Just brain dump. All you need to do is get it out of your head and onto the page (whether physical or digital).

But my boss won't let me. You don't need your boss's permission. If you take the day as a vacation day or personal time (PTO), they won't care one way or the other. Of course, if they're sold on the concept and convinced it will lead to greater productivity (see chap. 10), they may be happy to give you the time off or even let you use work time to complete it.

But my spouse won't let me. If your spouse doesn't want you to take a vacation day for Life Planning, it's because they don't (yet) appreciate its value. The truth is, your spouse will be the most immediate and direct beneficiary. But rather than try to convince your mate, ask him or her to read this book and then figure out how you can both take a day.

Here's the reality: Anything worthwhile is opposed. Steven Pressfield calls this the Resistance.[2] Any time you try to make an improvement or tackle a significant project, you can expect to encounter obstacles. Creating your Life Plan is no different. Sometimes these obstacles come from without; often they come from within. Regardless, the key is to connect with *why* your envisioned future is personally compelling, so you are willing to overcome the Resistance to achieve it.

How to Prepare for Your Time Away

Whether or not your Life Planning Day is productive depends largely on how well you prepare. We suggest you take these five actions.

1. *Block time on your calendar.* If you wait until a hole opens in your schedule, you'll never get around to it. (Don't ask us how we know this.) By that time, you might well have lost any sense of urgency too. Remember, what gets scheduled gets done.

Create a "Planning Retreat" appointment in your calendar and treat it like an important commitment—it is! If someone asks you to do something on that day, you can legitimately say, "I'm sorry, but I have a commitment then. How about [alternative date]?"

2. *Decide where to go.* It is essential that you get away from familiar surroundings. You want to be free of distractions. Doing this at work or home is not a good idea. You need a shift in perspective, and usually a change of scenery is necessary. Having said this, you don't have to go someplace exotic or expensive. We have done Life Planning at state parks, in cheap hotel rooms, in the public library, and in friends' vacation homes.

We know one woman, Beth, who goes to an inexpensive oceanside retreat center. She finds the beach puts her in exactly the frame of mind to reflect and plan. After one day away she comes back rested and ready for the next year.

Another man, Richard, goes to the Four Seasons. He plans all day, then invites his wife over for dinner and a night away from the kids. The first time he did it, his marriage wasn't in great shape. He set things back on the right course after that.

While we prefer to be outdoors, it isn't always possible or even necessary. The main thing is to find a place that is quiet, where you won't be distracted or interrupted. You also want to find a place you enjoy, a place that stimulates your creativity, your sensitivity, and your willingness to listen to the deeper desires of your heart.

3. *Take the necessary supplies.* You don't need much, but you will need a few items, starting with writing instruments. These could be a pen and yellow pad or journal, like a Moleskine notebook. Some people find that writing really connects their head and heart and allows them to dream big. Others prefer using their laptop. We've made templates for Microsoft Word and iWork Pages available at LivingForwardBook.com. Go with whatever you find most natural.

Make sure you have whatever you need to be mentally sharp and physically comfortable: the right clothes for the environment, water, snacks, and so on. You might also select some background music that will inspire you. Many people find movie scores and Focus@Will playlists especially helpful.

4. *Determine to be offline.* No phone, internet, apps—nothing, except whatever you're using to draft your Life Plan. We invite you to make a decision to be offline the whole day.

We know how difficult this is. We struggle with the temptation to stay connected too. But, we promise, being offline will not kill you. It might be a little tough during the first hour as you compulsively want to check your email or various social media accounts. But if you resist, the urge will pass. And it will set your mind free to do something you may not have done in years: *concentrate.*

Being offline will enable you to think deeply and reflectively. This is essential in creating a Life Plan that is both inspiring and practical. You can't do this if you opt for the quick fix that comes from checking email. Those distractions keep you from digging a little deeper to discover what you truly want and how you will achieve it.

5. *Enroll your family and colleagues.* Your family and the people you work with have legitimate needs. You're probably used to being responsive, but there are very few interruptions that can't wait for eight to ten hours.

The key is to warn people in advance that you'll be out-of-pocket. You don't have to provide many details. Just tell them you'll be inaccessible most of the day. Depending on how much your absence will affect your team, you might even meet with them before you unplug to address any questions or issues. You might also create a backup plan for any emergencies.

There may be other things you want to do in preparation for your Life Planning day, but these five should get you well on your way. The main thing is to be intentional and thoughtful as you approach it.

Maximizing Your Day

So now the big day has come. It may be one of the most pivotal days of your life to date. Are you ready to get started? Here are a few best practices we have gleaned from our own experience and those we have coached through the process.

Check Your Attitude

Before you actually start writing, we want to discuss your mind-set as you come to this exercise. Whatever your reality is, we recommend that you consciously shift your attitude and cultivate a spirit of gratitude, anticipation, and openness.

Gratitude is where every positive attitude starts. Negative emotions such as anger, fear, and sadness dissipate the moment you begin to be thankful. What can you be thankful for right now? Be thankful for everything you can possibly think of—your health, family, job, friends, community, whatever. Even if one of your Life Accounts is so seriously negative that you're not sure it can be salvaged, find something to be grateful for. Gratitude will allow you to create your Life Plan out of a sense of abundance, not scarcity. In our experience, people rarely get more of anything until they have learned to be grateful for what they already have.

Anticipation is the exact opposite of dread. It means leaning into this experience, embracing it, and playing full out. In life, you often get what you expect. If you expect to get insight, wisdom, and inspiration, you will likely find them. If you expect boredom, confusion, or frustration, you will likely find them as well. What is your expectation today? It's worth taking the time to notice your expectations and shift them, if necessary, toward a positive focus.

Finally, we suggest you cultivate *openness*. This will mean different things to different people. Generally, we mean you should approach this day without assumptions. Be willing to explore your intuitions and listen to what your heart is saying—you're creating the necessary room for it to speak for a reason. Be willing to be surprised. Some of the greatest insights we have ever experienced were those we least expected. We hear the same from those we coach.

Remind Yourself of the Goal

It's worth remembering why you have come here. Focus on the deliverable--what do you want to leave with when you are done? Your goal is to create a written Life Plan, using the format we have shared with you in chapters 4–7. It can be anywhere from five to fifteen pages. Most are usually less than ten, but the only thing that matters is that it works for you.

By the day's end, you want at least a first draft of each of the three major sections that make up the Life Plan. Even better, set a goal to have enough time left in the day to review and tweak it. The next day, you want to start implementing your plan. You can't do that unless your plan is complete. That's why you need to focus on the deliverable—a complete, written Life Plan.

Trust the Process

This is difficult to do, especially the first time. The Process doesn't always follow a predictable path. Maybe you'll start out with a burst of energy, get stuck, and want to quit. That sometimes happens. Don't despair. Keep your head in the game. Maybe it's the opposite. You arrive distracted or discouraged and have a difficult time getting started. The same advice holds. Don't despair. Trust the process.

After coaching thousands of people through this process, we can guarantee that you will finish this day with a completed Life Plan if you just stay engaged and keep putting one foot in front of the other.

Listen to Your Heart

As you commit your thoughts to the page, notice what you feel. Does what you just wrote for this or that Life Account resonate? Does it leave you flat? Ring hollow? If so, consider an alternative.

I (Michael) took my annual Life Planning day shortly before stepping down as the CEO of Thomas Nelson. For months I'd been restless. I felt change on the horizon but was enjoying the comfort of my position. Turning to my career account, I wrote, "Taking the company to the next level." But the words just sat there, and the more I looked at them, the more lifeless and uninspired they seemed. I felt *no energy* around the statement.

So I gave myself permission to dream. *What do I wish I could be doing if money or status were not an issue?* Almost immediately the thought came: *Speak and write full-time.* I had no idea how I would make it happen, but I knew it was the right course. I chose to listen to my heart and began to lay the groundwork for one of the biggest career transitions I would ever experience.

Don't Worry about Getting It Perfect

Please, please, please listen to us when we say this: perfectionism is the mother of procrastination. If you expect perfection, you will never finish.

Remember, your Life Plan will likely never be published. No one will grade it. It's not for public consumption. This document is *for you.* So permit yourself to be less than perfect. You can use bad grammar, incomplete sentences, or badly formatted paragraphs. It doesn't have to be perfect—just meaningful to you.

Stay Focused

You will be tempted to become distracted, especially when the going gets tough. This is normal. It reminds us of

Dug, the talking dog in the movie *Up*. Right in the middle of an intense conversation, he sees something move, shouts "Squirrel!" and dashes off to chase it. Whenever you feel that urge, resist it. Stay put, stay focused, and the distraction will eventually pass. This is not to say you shouldn't take breaks. Take as many as you need to be effective.

One way to handle those fleeting thoughts is to keep a separate pad of paper for stray ideas—a parking lot for all those random things you might want to return to later but which will derail you now.

If you follow the practices we recommend here, you will come out the other end of the chute with a Life Plan that gives your life purpose and direction, along with the inspiration necessary to start the journey.

Time to Step Up

You are now at a critical juncture. You can put this book down, blow off what you have learned, and continue to drift. Go that way and you'll never experience the benefits of Life Planning. Who knows where you might end up? But chances are, it won't be a destination you would have picked.

Alternatively, you can roll up your sleeves and get started. We're not asking you to write the Great American Novel, a doctoral dissertation, or even an essay. We're asking you to think, imagine, and write on something you already care deeply about: *your life*. In the next several chapters we'll talk about some important aspects of *implementing* your plan. But for now, the most important thing for you to do is to set the date. When will you create your plan?

Thousands before you have done it. You can too.

Part Three

MAKE IT HAPPEN

8

Implement Your Plan

Strategy without execution is hallucination!
—Mike Roach

The big day is behind you—now it's time to act. If you want the benefit of a Life Plan, you have to implement it. Your Action Plans need to be scheduled into your normal day-to-day routine. But what if you have no additional time? What if, as you review your calendar, you realize you're maxed out and don't have room for one more thing?

Despite all of our gadgets and apps, we don't have more time. Most of us are only getting busier. Most of us work considerably more than forty hours a week, handling calls in the car, emails at night, and projects on the weekend. One survey found that many professionals with smartphones engaged with their work more than seventy hours each week!

119

That doesn't even begin to factor in our family and social commitments.[1]

Sometimes our lives feel like the famous scene from *I Love Lucy* when Lucy and Ethel got jobs in a candy factory. We're standing at the conveyor belt, wrapping chocolates as they come down the line, but there are too many, coming too fast. If we miss even one, we're in trouble, but we can't keep up. Pretty soon we're stuffing chocolates wherever they'll fit, hoping no one will find out. And here's the bad news. The better we get at hiding all our unwrapped chocolates, the more competent we appear, and our managers just send more chocolates our way.

If you feel overwhelmed by life's demands, you're not alone. But if we are to achieve what we said we wanted in our Life Plan, we must fight the drift and swim against the current.

In 2012, I (Michael) faced this situation again for the umpteenth time. My book, *Platform*, was about to hit shelves, my speaking calendar was stuffed with events, and one of my daughters was getting married in a month's time. I was swamped, and it felt like I was falling further and further behind. Something had to give. Fortunately this wasn't my first rodeo. I had a set of tools I could use to get the breathing room I needed.

We want to share these tools with you in this chapter. Let's start by looking at your calendar.

How Much Margin Do You Have?

Realistically, do you have time to keep up with what you have been doing *plus* build in additional time to achieve the Action Plans you created in your Life Plan? Probably not.

Maybe you've said something like this to yourself or your spouse:

- "As soon as I get acclimated to this new job, I will have some breathing room."
- "As soon as I get my toddler into school, I will have more time to do other things."
- "As soon as my spouse finishes his current work assignment, I will have some help with the kids."

But before you know it, weeks turn into months, months turn into years. People go from one "temporary situation" to the next. Before long it's permanent. Like the proverbial frog in the kettle, you've been boiled, one degree at a time.

What we desperately need is *margin*—time to breathe, to reflect, to act. How does the lack of margin make you feel? Anxious? Frustrated? Overwhelmed? Conversely, how does margin make you feel? Relaxed? Focused? Present? If you are to be successful with your Life Plan, you must create more margin so you have room for what's important, not merely urgent.

Margin is possible. But it requires you to recognize the forces that threaten to gobble it up and then enact the appropriate countermeasures. It specifically requires that you learn and practice three skills: triaging your calendar, scheduling your priorities, and saying no to more requests. Let's take these one at a time.

1. Triage Your Calendar

Triage is a military term. In a battle zone, medics must decide where to apply their limited resources. They can't help everyone. Medical personnel recognize that some patients will survive without medical care, while others won't survive even if they get care. Triage means ignoring these two groups and focusing on those who will only survive *with* appropriate medical care. It's a tough sort, but that's how they maximize survivor rates and win wars.

With regard to your calendar, triage means you must know which things you can safely cancel or reschedule, and which ones demand your participation. Again, the goal is to create ample margin to execute the Action Plans you have included in your Life Plan. Here's how it works:

- *Protect the basics.* Review your current appointments and ask how they relate to your list of Life Account priorities. Are they essential in helping you to advance toward your envisioned future? If so, leave them in your calendar. If not, consider canceling or rescheduling (see below).

- *Eliminate the nonessentials.* Sometimes we make commitments that seem important when we schedule them. We get caught up in the enthusiasm of a new idea or project. After further reflection, we realize they aren't really that important. So, to the extent possible, we need to either cancel these meetings or see if we can handle them another way.

- *Reschedule some of what remains.* Some things are important, but they are not important *now*. Most of us like to get things done as soon as possible, but this sometimes works against us. So we need to review our calendars and see what can be postponed without significant consequences.

Practicing triage will help free up your calendar, giving you back some of the margin you need to achieve what matters most. But triage alone is not enough.

2. Schedule Your Priorities

The goal here is not simply having fewer commitments—though that would be a welcome relief for most of us—but the *right* commitments. If life is a juggling act, the important skill is knowing which balls are rubber and which are crystal. We suggest two tools: the Ideal Week and Annual Time Block.

Your Ideal Week

We were first introduced to this concept by author Todd Duncan in a series of audio recordings he made that eventually became the book *Time Traps: Proven Strategies for Swamped Salespeople.* The idea is similar to a financial budget. The only difference is that you plan how you will spend your time rather than your money. And like a financial budget, you spend it on paper first.

Your Ideal Week—the week you would live if you could control 100 percent of what happens—is divided into a simple grid. Each day has a *theme.* In addition, each day is segmented according to a specific *focus area.* We use a simple spreadsheet to do this. It looks similar to the example from Tim in figure 8.1.

You can see Tim's *themes* are listed on the very top row:

- Monday is devoted to his team, one-on-one meetings, and a staff lunch.
- Tuesday and Wednesday are devoted to travel and extended meetings (e.g., Monthly Business Review meetings).
- Thursday is an ad hoc day. This is where Tim pushes external requests for meetings.
- Friday is spent on planning and long-term thinking.

FIGURE 8.1

EXAMPLE OF AN IDEAL WEEK

Themes		Teams	Travel & Extended Meetings	
		Mon	Tues	Wed
Self	05:00–05:30			Quiet Time
	05:30–06:00			Reading
	06:00–06:30	Chest & Back	Cardio	Lower Body
	06:30–07:00			
	07:00–07:30			Shower & Dress
	07:30–08:00			Process Email
	08:00–08:30			Commute
Work	08:30–09:00			
	09:00–09:30	Direct Report #1		
	09:30–10:00			
	10:00–10:30			
	10:30–11:00	Direct Report #2	Week 1: Travel	
	11:00–11:30			
	11:30–12:00			
	12:00–12:30	Lunch Huddle	Week 2: Financial Reviews	
	12:30–01:00			
	01:00–10:30		Week 3: Travel	
	01:30–02:00	Direct Report #3		
	02:00–02:30			
	02:30–03:00		Week 4: Ad Hoc Meetings	
	03:00–03:30	Direct Report #4		
	03:30–04:00			
	04:00–04:30			
	04:30–05:00			
	05:00–05:30			Process Email
	05:30–06:00			Planning for Tomorrow
	06:00–06:30			Commute
Family & Other	06:30–07:00			Dinner with Gail
	07:00–07:30			
	07:30–08:00			
	08:00–08:30			Writing
	08:30–09:00			

Ad Hoc	Planning	Personal	Church
Thu	Fri	Sat	Sun
Cardio	Arms & Shoulders	Cardio	Sunday School Prep
		Read	
		Household Chores	Shower
			Commute
Available for Ad Hoc Meetings	Available for Ad Hoc Meetings	Review Personal Finances	Sunday School
			Church
Available for Lunch Meetings	Available for Lunch Meetings		Lunch with Family
		Lunch	Commute
Available for Ad Hoc Meetings	Review Business Vision and Business Plan		
Process Email		Vespers	
Planning for Tomorrow			
Commute			
	Date with Gail		Weekly Review & Planning

- Saturday is for personal chores and activities.
- Sunday is for church, rest, and planning the next week.

Tim's *focus areas* are listed in the left-most column:

- The early morning hours are devoted to self: reading, praying, and working out.
- The middle of the day is devoted to work. Tim arrives at the office by 8:30 a.m. and leaves promptly at 6:00 p.m. It is amazing what you can get done in the time allotted when you create "hard boundaries" around your work. Otherwise, Parkinson's Law becomes operative: "Work expands to the time allotted for it."
- The end of the day is reserved for Tim's family and relaxing. Currently, he has three children living at home. Eating dinner together is a huge priority. It gives the family time to connect and catch up. He and his wife then enjoy reading for the last thirty minutes of the day.

Note that activities contributing to Tim's priorities on his Life Plan are shaded light gray. Those not related to his priorities are shaded dark. Those that could be either are white. The diagonally lined periods are simply not scheduled and represent "margin." This scheme is admittedly subjective, but it enables most people to ensure they are working on what matters most.

To use this tool, we suggest that you map out your own Ideal Week. You can either download our Excel spreadsheet at LivingForwardBook.com/ideal-week or start from scratch. Once you have created your Ideal Week, you can use this document as a basic template for planning. It is also helpful if you give it to your assistant or colleagues, so that everyone is working with the same expectations and toward the same goals.

Not everything can be shoehorned into this template. However, having this document will better enable you to accomplish what matters most.

Your Annual Time Block

Another tool that we have found helpful is an Annual Time Block. This enables you to plan your life three years in advance. Obviously, we are not talking about all the little details. Our lives are too dynamic for that to work.

But this tool enables you to "put the big rocks" into your calendar first, so the important is not overwhelmed by the urgent. The best way to do this is to claim your calendar before someone else does.

Unfortunately, none of the current calendar tools we are familiar with offer the kind of annual view we wanted. With commercial products now available, the most you can see is a one-month view. So, we created an Annual Time Block tool in Excel. It also includes an example of a current calendar. You can enter the year you want to schedule in cell A5, and the calendar will automatically recalculate. It even takes into account leap years. You can download it at LivingForwardBook.com.

Begin by scheduling the most nondiscretionary things and moving to the most discretionary things. Typically, we recommend updating this calendar somewhere in the fourth quarter of the year. You might consider adding to your Annual Time Block in this order:

1. Birthdays and Anniversaries
2. Holidays

3. Industry Events
4. Vacations
5. Board Meetings
6. Business Review Meetings
7. Special Trips
8. Time with Friends

Your list may differ. The issue is to grab the dates while you can before someone else does. We would rather have other people plan around our priorities than be forced to plan around theirs. Remember: If you don't have a plan for your life, someone else does.

The key is balance. Make sure you schedule time for the things that are important to you. Otherwise you will find yourself scrambling to find time for your priorities. If you are not careful, you will wake up one day and discover that you have spent your life living for other people's priorities. To prevent that from happening, we also need to learn to say no a lot more often. Let's talk about how.

3. Learn to Say No with Grace

Do you have a difficult time saying no? The Jim Carrey movie *Yes Man* is about a man whose life goes nowhere until he learns to say yes to everything. Suddenly, his luck turns around—for a while. It eventually catches up to him, just like it catches up to all of us. Most of us hate disappointing others, but at some point, you realize that you can't say yes to everything. Attempting to do so risks your own priorities and what matters most.

In his bestselling book, *The Power of a Positive No: How to Say No and Still Get to Yes*, Harvard professor William

Ury offers three responses to someone who asks us to do something we don't want to do:

1. *Accommodation*: We say yes when we want to say no. This usually comes when we value the relationship of the person making the request above the importance of our own interests.

2. *Attack*: We say no poorly. This is a result of valuing our own interests above the importance of the relationship. Sometimes we are fearful or resentful of the request and overreact to the person asking.

3. *Avoidance*: We say nothing at all. Because we are afraid of offending the other party, we avoid the situation, hoping the problem will go away. It rarely does.

Sometimes these responses spill over into one another, making a difficult situation worse. For example, perhaps we initially avoid the request, prompting a second or third request. We then get annoyed and attack the one making the request. This leads to guilt, perhaps an apology, and then accommodation.

Fortunately there is a better way. Dr. Ury suggests a fourth strategy that he names a "positive no." A positive no helps us avoid sacrificing either the relationship or our priorities. This simple strategy employs a "Yes-No-Yes" formula. "In contrast to an ordinary No which begins with a No and ends with a No," Dr. Ury explains, "a positive No begins with a Yes and ends with a Yes."[2] Here is how the three elements work together:

Yes: A positive no begins by saying yes to yourself and protecting what is important to you. We would add the importance of affirming the person making the request.

No: It then continues with a matter-of-fact no that sets clear boundaries. We recommend that you avoid leaving the door open by saying "maybe," as in "maybe I can say yes to your request in the future."

Yes: A positive no ends with a yes that affirms the relationship and offers another solution to the person's request.

For example, I (Michael) often receive email messages from aspiring authors, asking me to review their book proposals. This is the result of having spent most of my career in the publishing field. Here's how I respond using the Yes-No-Yes formula.[3]

Bill,

Congratulations on your new proposal! Very few authors make it this far. Thanks for your interest in having me review it.

Unfortunately, due to my other commitments, I am no longer able to review book proposals. Therefore, I must decline.

However, I can give you some guidance on how to get published. If you haven't already done so, may I recommend that you start by reading my blog post, "Advice for First Time Authors." In it, I offer step-by-step instructions for what to do first.

I also have published an entire audio course called "Get Published," which distills my 30-plus years of publishing experience into twenty-one learning sessions.

I hope you will find this helpful.

With best wishes for your publishing success,

Michael

Few people ever press further after receiving an email like this. They typically respond by saying, "Thanks for your consideration. I understand. Thanks for getting back to me." The people we coach get this intuitively after a while. Yes and no are like yin and yang. Start looking at your accounts. When you say yes to a nonpriority request, you're potentially saying no to your friends, children, spouse, not to mention your own health and spiritual growth. "You have to say no to some things if you are truly prioritizing your marriage and your family," said one of our clients, a Chick-fil-A executive. And he's right. You're saying no to one thing so you can say yes to something else.

Conclusion

Your time is a zero-sum game. When you say yes to one thing, you are simultaneously saying no to something else. The more successful you become in life and work, the more difficult saying no becomes. You find yourself saying no to good things—worthy things—in order to say yes to your most important priorities.

If you are to successfully implement your Life Plan, you must take these three actions: triage your calendar, schedule your priorities, and learn to say no with grace.

9

Keep It Alive

Self-discipline is the ability to make yourself do something you don't necessarily want to do, to get a result you would really like to have.

—Andy Andrews

A plan is worthless unless you review it on a regular basis. Once you have completed your Life Plan, it's important to establish a pattern of regular review.

Years ago I (Michael) was part of a rapidly growing organization. Finally we got to the place where the CEO determined we needed a strategic plan. At a staff meeting he announced, "The days of 'winging it' are over. We need a formal plan, and we need it *now*." He then hired a very expensive strategic planning consultant and scheduled a three-day retreat.

About fifty members of the company leadership, representing different departments and interest, gathered at a gorgeous resort facility outside Austin, Texas. The consultant led the assembled team through the process. It was extremely thorough and systematic. He had custom, leather-bound three-ring binders created with the name of our company stamped on the cover and multicolored tabs inside. The team had incredible discussions, made important decisions, and achieved alignment on key issues that had dogged them for years. They created detailed action plans with milestones, due dates, and accountabilities. The plan was a work of art.

The only problem was they never looked at the plan again—ever. Every executive at the retreat had the plan on a shelf in his or her office, but it was never reviewed, tweaked, or revised. This is nothing new in corporate life. A company that creates and then implements a plan is the exception rather than the rule.

We don't want this to happen when it comes to your Life Plan. We want to ensure you implement it. The only way this is possible is if you have a process in place for making it *visible*. You need to review, tweak, and revise it regularly if it is to actually shape your life.

Dr. Henry Cloud explains the importance of this process in *Boundaries for Leaders*. Achieving our goals depends on giving them attention. When we do that, important things are addressed, while unimportant things are not. In the process we generate vivid awareness of what's required to achieve our goals—what Dr. Cloud calls "working memory." Reviewing your Life Plan will help expand your working memory and thereby increase the chances you'll achieve your goals. We'd like to suggest three ways you can do this.

Start by Reading Your Plan Daily

At Building Champions, we coach our clients to read their Life Plan daily in the morning for the first ninety days. You should also read it out loud. The idea is to lock each aspect of your plan into your heart and mind and to avoid this exercise from becoming rote.

Review Your Plan Weekly

After the first ninety days, the next way to keep your plan alive is to practice what some have called "The Weekly Review." This is an opportunity to get your head above the daily blizzard of activities and see where you've been and where you're going. It's also an opportunity to see how you are progressing against what matters most—those items you have identified in your Life Plan.

In our practice the Weekly Review is the key to staying atop our projects and assignments. The result is that we stay in control of our workload and keep moving forward in the direction of our most important priorities.

No one has written more compellingly about the importance of the Weekly Review than productivity expert David Allen. In his book *Getting Things Done*, he writes:

> Many of us seem to have it in our natures consistently to entangle ourselves in more than we have the ability to handle. We book ourselves in back to back meetings all day, go to after-hours events and generate ideas and commitments we need to deal with, and get embroiled in engagements and projects that have the potential to spin our creative intelligence into cosmic orbits.

The whirlwind of activity is precisely what makes the Weekly Review so valuable. It builds in some capturing, re-evaluation, and reprocessing time to keep you in balance. There is simply no way to do this necessary regrouping while you're trying to get everyday work done.[1]

I (Michael) usually do my weekly review on Friday when I have clarity about what got done and what's still pending. I used to do it on Sunday night so I was clear going into the new week, but I've since come to see the value of being completely off Saturday and Sunday. By doing it Friday, I'm clear about what's coming on Monday and I'm free to fully engage in rest over the weekend.

I (Daniel) prefer to do my weekly review at home as well but early Monday mornings. It helps me to focus on what matters most before I head to the office and jump into the demands of my week.

But the truth is that any day can work. Some people we coach like to do a weekly review on Friday afternoon, at the end of their workweek. Others prefer first thing Monday morning. The important thing is that you are intentional about it and actually put an appointment on your calendar to do it.

We generally recommend fifteen to thirty minutes for your Weekly Review—but it could go longer if necessary. It will rarely require the full time you set aside, but it's helpful to have the window blocked off on your schedule. If you don't schedule it, it's easy to avoid this activity or schedule something else in this slot.

What should you do during this time? It's not essential, but here's the "agenda" we recommend and use. It considers more than your Life Plan, but it is all interrelated. It is modified from David Allen's list. Feel free to customize as you like:[2]

1. *Review your Life Plan.* Read through your Life Plan, word for word. Keep in mind, it's a brief document so it really doesn't take long to go through it. The value is that it gives you a high-level view, so you don't lose touch with what matters most. It also infuses your daily actions with purpose.

2. *Gather all loose papers and process.* Empty everything out of your briefcase or computer case, your physical inbox, and your wallet or purse. Then go through each piece of paper and decide what to do with it. Following David Allen's model, first ask if it is something that requires action. If not, you have three options. You can

   • trash it,
   • add it to your Someday/Maybe list, or
   • file it for future reference.

   If the item requires action, you can
   • do it immediately if the action takes less than two minutes or add it to a task list to do later;
   • defer it by actually scheduling a time on your calendar to deal with it; or
   • delegate it to someone else for action and enter it into your task list. We use a "Pending" or "Waiting For" category. (This is just another way to label those tasks that await input from someone else before you can move forward.)

3. *Process your notes.* Note taking is a critical productivity skill.[3] You can use a low-tech solution, like a Moleskine notebook, or a high-tech one, like Evernote, on your desktop, tablet, or smartphone. It doesn't matter.

The important thing is to read back through your notes, looking for action items that you agreed to do. You want to transfer these to a task list.

4. *Review previous calendar data.* We suggest you review the previous week's meetings in your calendar program and see if there is anything you missed. For example, you may not take notes in lunch meetings, but you might want to follow up with a thank-you note or a gift. Reviewing the prior week's appointments provides an opportunity to stimulate your memory and catch things you might otherwise miss.

5. *Review upcoming calendar.* This is one of the most important parts of the Weekly Review. This is an opportunity for you to note any upcoming meetings with an eye to the preparation you might need to do. This keeps you ahead of the curve and your assignments on track. (We are still amazed at how many professionals show up at a meeting without reviewing their previous assignments. This makes them look sloppy and incompetent. Reality is that they don't have a process in place for systematic review of previous meetings and assignments.)

6. *Review your Action lists.* Although we recommend and do this on a daily basis, the focus is broader during the Weekly Review. We ask ourselves, "What do we really need to accomplish this week?" If it's a really important task, we drag it onto our calendar and schedule it.

7. *Review your Pending (e.g., "Waiting For") list.* This is a list of items you have delegated to others and are important enough to track. If something is overdue, or if it needs a progress update, you can send an email or

make a phone call and nudge the person responsible. We also recommend you make a note in the task itself that you have sent a reminder.

8. *Review Project lists.* When an action consists of many subactions, it qualifies as a project. For example, planning the annual staff retreat may require multiple actions, like reserving a venue, booking a caterer, sending invitations, and so on. Whatever project management system you use, the important thing is to review your major projects and consider the next action required to keep the ball rolling.

9. *Review Someday/Maybe lists.* These are items that don't require immediate action but would be nice to do someday. This is a great place to park ideas you don't want to forget but are not quite ready to commit to. Once you are ready, you can transfer the item to the appropriate action list.

Our readers, clients, and seminar attendees tell us that the Weekly Review is the most important tool they have in their quest to implement their Life Plan. We agree, but it's important to remember that this is one possible review strategy. It's effective for us, but others use different methods. The point is to find a system that works for you. Our hope is that you'll find some useful handles here so you can stay accountable to your Life Plan.

Tweak Your Plan Quarterly

The secret to staying atop your priorities is to schedule regular times for review and reflection. But there also needs to be a time to revise your plan or "true it up" to reality. Dr. Cloud says this kind of purposeful engagement is what enables people to soar.

While you can do this tactically in your Weekly Review, you should do this regularly in a more in-depth, strategic fashion as well. We recommend you do a formal, scheduled Quarterly Review.

This appointment-with-yourself is basically an extended version of the Weekly Review. In the Weekly Review you climb to the tops of the trees and peer at the forest. In the Quarterly Review you take a hot air balloon to a thousand feet or so to see how the forest fits into the overall landscape.

A Quarterly Review is a great way to ensure you stay on track. You can make incremental adjustments rather than lose an entire year before realizing you're off course. How you do it depends on your personality. The artist and scientist will do it differently. But the point remains the same no matter how you approach it—to invest time in being more intentional.

If possible, we recommend that you try to leave the office or your workday environment for your Quarterly Review. You want to get away from phones, drop-in visitors, and the hustle and bustle of office life. Of course, you could also do this on a Saturday morning. You may want to be in the same place you worked on your Life Plan day. It doesn't have to be fancy, just relatively private and quiet.

Think through the agenda before you begin. Based on our practice, following are two items you might want to consider:

Review your Life Plan. We encourage you to read through your plan one time without editing. Then begin the revision process. You might tweak the language in your Purpose Statement or Envisioned Future. You might add a Bible verse or inspirational quote. Most importantly, completely reassess your Current Realities and draft Specific Commitments. Try to do this part of the exercise as though it were your first time through the Life Planning exercise.

Write goals for the upcoming quarter. Then we recommend you take the review of your Life Plan and translate it into specific, ninety-day goals or objectives. We are not asking you to create a long list of to-do items. That's too tactical for this exercise. Instead, we recommend a short list of the five to seven most important goals you can accomplish in the next quarter to move the needle on your Plan.

If you are committed to a Quarterly Review, we strongly suggest you schedule these far, far in advance—about two years out. If you wait until you have a break in your schedule, you'll never get to it. Making appointments with yourself and scheduling other things around them is the key to proactive self-management.

Revise Your Plan Yearly

The Weekly Review is essential. The Quarterly Review is helpful. But if you really want to keep your Life Plan alive, an Annual Review is critical. This is a time to take an extended look at your plan, evaluate what you have accomplished over the past year, and determine where you want to go in the next.

Writing your Life Plan for the first time is the biggest challenge for nearly everyone. But once you have it, it is much easier to revise. You have already done the heavy lifting!

We recommend a day in the last quarter of the year to do a "deep dive" on your Life Plan. (In the previous chapter, we also recommended updating your Annual Time Block.) Doing this can replace your final Quarterly Review. The only difference between the Quarterly Review and the Annual Review is the amount of time you have to reflect and revise.

During this time, it is worth questioning your previous assumptions:

Outcomes

- Is there anyone (person or group) missing from your list?
- Anyone you want to delete?
- Anything you want to change about how you hope to be remembered?

Priorities

- Do you want to add any new Life Accounts to this section?
- Are there any you should delete because they are no longer relevant?
- Have your priorities changed? If so, do these need to be arranged to reflect that?

Action Plans

- Do you need to create new Action Plans for new Life Accounts?
- Does the Envisioned Future for each account still resonate with you? Could it be more expressive? Do you "see" anything differently than what you originally envisioned?
- What about the Purpose Statement for each account? Could it be tightened?
- What about your Current Reality? What have you accomplished this past year that you are proudest of?

What do you feel you should have been acknowledged for but weren't? What disappointments or regrets did you experience this past year?

One of my (Daniel) favorite weeks of the year is the week between Christmas and New Years. I have the privilege of closing the office and taking the week off to celebrate, reflect, and recharge prior to the chapter change into the year ahead. And one of my favorite days during this special week is spent in a little cabin on the Oregon Coast. It is usually crazy stormy and the perfect setting to light a fire, make a hot pot of tea and to focus on what matters most. This is where I take a full day to review my Life Plan and the lessons of the previous year. I then make the changes to my Life Plan for the year ahead.

Whether you change your Life Plan a little or a lot doesn't matter, provided it reflects your life as you want it to be. Some years, you might change it more. Some years, less. Much of it depends on what has transpired in the previous year and where you hope to go in the next.

Conclusion

"Work feels like I'm in a rat race," Stan told us. But when we asked him about family and the rest of his life, he said those accounts were at an excellent 9.5. Considering how hectic things are, it would be easy and understandable for Stan to turn more focus to his job. But he's holding the line. When asked, he said that the Life Plan shows him how much to invest in each area of his life. It helps him keep balance—particularly since he reviews it regularly. That's the difference maker. In fact, he told us, he has not "seen another way for people to follow through."

Stan's results have been so beneficial, he's got his whole family doing it now, including his parents and siblings.

A few years ago, I (Michael) changed my Life Plan more than in any of the previous ten years. But that was largely due to my life circumstances changing so significantly. The last of our five daughters moved out. I transitioned out of my role as the chairman and CEO of Thomas Nelson Publishers. I launched my new career as an online training provider. I had a whole new set of business associates.

Thankfully many of my Life Accounts didn't change—my spiritual, physical, intellectual, and avocation accounts stayed largely the same. I only tweaked them slightly. But given my new life circumstances, I needed to make adjustments to my family and professional accounts. I wanted—and needed—a Life Plan that was compelling. The Weekly, Quarterly, and Annual Reviews we have suggested here ensured that I was constantly moving toward a future I wanted to embrace.

10

Join a Revolution

They always say time changes things, but you actually have to change them yourself.

—Andy Warhol

A work-related crisis can affect our health, our family, and our finances. And the reverse is true too. A family, health, or financial crisis can impact our work. The quantity and quality of our output may suffer. Projects can slip. Budgets may be missed. Colleagues—who often don't have much margin themselves—are forced to fill in the gaps.

Here's the reality: Your personal life is a myth. There is no such thing as a compartmentalized life. Every area, space, category, and set of relationships is interrelated. You are a seamless whole.

When the Great Recession hit, I (Michael) experienced this firsthand as the CEO of Thomas Nelson. As mentioned before, the company went through several layoffs to survive the fallout. The executive team searched for other solutions. They haggled with suppliers, postponed purchases, slashed expenses, and fought daily to keep the boat afloat and moving forward. But there seemed to be no end in sight. No one can turn off this kind of stress with the office lights. We brought all that stress and worry home, negatively affecting our families and health.

We realize that events in one area of our lives cascade into every other area. While a Life Plan can't protect us from the impact of something as global as the recession, it can help us avoid many self-inflicted wounds. At least three very important ideas are connected to the realization that you cannot compartmentalize your life.

The first is something we said at the start: Self-leadership always precedes team leadership. Leaders who build cultures and organizations that make the greatest difference are highly self-aware and well rounded; they invest time into several accounts and live lives that are attractive to those they serve and lead.

The second is that our teams are watching us. They set their levels of trust and engagement based on what they see in our lives. How we leaders live matters.

Many leaders we have worked with have excelled in using their Life Plans to help them improve how they influence and lead. But unfortunately others never created plans for their lives or abandoned them to focus on just their professional or financial accounts. So again, who we are, the decisions we make, our investments of time, talents, and treasures will show those around us what we value most.

The third is this: What's true for you is true for your team members. They can't compartmentalize their lives either. The first two points should color the third, which is the focus of this chapter: How you can use the Life Planning process to empower your people and strengthen your organization.

The Business Benefits of Life Planning

Companies across the globe are beginning to see that one's personal life and work life are inseparable. Many are encouraging their employees to develop written Life Plans and giving them the training they need to do so. These companies are benefiting in three specific ways:

1. *Helping employees do Life Planning communicates your care.* Employees working for you have dreams, hopes, and aspirations. When you encourage Life Planning, you are essentially saying, "We want to help you accomplish your ultimate goals and dreams. We know that involves your job, but we also know it is more than what you do while at work."

Chick-fil-A has been a wonderful client of Building Champions for many years. The relationship started with our coaching just a few leaders in their organization. It has grown into hundreds of coaching relationships. Their leadership has been so impacted by Life Planning that it is now a part of the training for all new restaurant owners. Several times a year one of our coaches will join them to walk groups of new owners through the process of creating their own Life Plans. They absolutely believe that self-leadership always precedes team leadership.

Similarly, Marc Laird, CEO of the national mortgage banking firm Cornerstone Home Lending, decided several years ago that the personal gains he received from the Life Planning process could benefit his employees. So Building

Champions helped him craft a strategy to roll out Life Planning to his more than one thousand teammates. Cornerstone had a Building Champions coach come to their larger markets to walk their teammates and key clients through the process. Marc also recorded videos for all new hires, encouraging them to take a paid day off to create their plans. He also had me (Daniel) record several Life Planning videos that are now stored on their intranet as a team resource. Additionally, Marc had Building Champions assist with team challenges and help his teammates to live out their plans.

Todd Salmans, CEO of Prime Lending, is another leader who sees Life Planning as key to building a high-performing team. His organization subsidized the investment of Building Champions coaching for hundreds of their teammates. They also partnered with Building Champions to create a private four-day Coaching Experience for 250 of their managers and leaders. Everyone spends the first day just working through their Life Plans.

And here's one more valuable story about using Life Planning to care for the people who work with you: Brian McKay is the vice president and chief operating officer at SC Telco Federal Credit Union in Greenville, South Carolina. He became a Life Planner in 2011 after reading about it on my (Michael's) blog. It had such a radical impact on his own life that he shared it with other executives at the corporate office, including his CEO Steve Harkins, who immediately saw the potential for the entire workforce.

They brought me in to the annual all-employee meeting to provide a three-hour training session for everyone—from the executive suite to the mailroom. Following the meeting, Brian appointed a steering committee to promote Life

Planning in the organization, using the company newsletter to recount stories of employees who were succeeding at Life Planning. They offered small group assistance and support. They answered questions as they came up. A year later SC Telco invited me back for a follow-up session at the annual all-employee meeting. In addition to doing a review and sharing best practices, I interviewed two employees with significant Life Planning success stories. "The biggest takeaway for me in the Life Planning process is knowing I am working for a company that wants me to be happy and productive in every area of my life," said one, a compliance officer with the bank. "That's a gift!"

2. *Helping employees do Life Planning ensures they are productive at work.* When employees engage in Life Planning, they are less likely to have something like a health crisis or marital conflict distract them at work. They can be more fully present on the job and focus on tasks at hand.

Dr. Melanie Lankau of Wake Forest University partnered with Building Champions to assess the impact of coaching. One of the key findings of her research—which was no surprise to us—is that "Life Satisfaction is positively correlated with job satisfaction and all performance measures." Said another way, those who feel satisfied with their personal lives are more satisfied with their careers and perform better.

3. *Helping employees do Life Planning empowers them to be engaged on the job.* When employees are working to attain passion and progress in every area of life, they are less likely to be cynical or apathetic. They have the emotional resources to invest in their work and the customers they serve.

We have heard from countless clients that after completing their Life Plans they are more focused, present, and engaged at work. They are not worried about what they are not doing or should be doing in the other critical areas of their lives, because their Life Plan provides the framework for dealing with those as well. It provides the structure that frees them to give attention to their teammates, customers, projects, and tasks without distracting thoughts or the guilt of neglecting another area of their lives.

And here's why that's ultimately important: When employees feel valued, and are more productive and engaged, they create a culture that can truly be a strategic advantage in today's competitive environment.

The Corporate Implementation Process

Hopefully, by now you are convinced that Life Planning could benefit your organization. We'd like to share seven best practices for implementing it.

1. *Practice before you preach.* St. Francis of Assisi reportedly said, "Preach the gospel at all times and when necessary use words." Nothing speaks louder than our lives. When we preach what we aren't practicing, people consider us hypocrites. That's hardly the outcome we're after.

On the other hand, when we practice what we preach— especially *before* we preach it—we provide evidence that what we are advocating actually works. We've all had this experience when a friend or co-worker decides to lose weight. Their strategy is far more compelling *after* they have lost fifty pounds.

2. *Get your leadership team on board.* Alignment is essential in any major, corporate-wide initiative, but it is especially relevant here. Some executives have been conditioned to believe that there needs to be clear distinction between

one's personal and work lives. As long as they believe this, it will be difficult to get their support.

This is why we usually advise a staged rollout. Buy the book for your executive team first. Get them enrolled in the process. Bring in outside training if necessary. You want your leadership team familiar with the process and also practicing it before attempting to implement it throughout the workforce.

But here's a caution: Make it optional. We have seen the strategy backfire when it is rolled out as a mandate instead of an invite. In connection to point 1 above, it has been most successfully implemented when the changes in the leader's life become noticeable and his passion for Life Planning causes those around him to want what he has.

3. *Set aside a half day for training.* This is where it starts to get fun. This is also where you begin to communicate to teammates that you are serious about this Life Planning stuff and willing to put money where your mouth is. You can provide this training in one of three ways. We have arranged these from least to most expensive:

- Teach through the book using the Group Study Guide (found online at LivingForwardBook.com).
- Buy the Living Forward Experience Training Course and guide employees through it.
- Bring in one of our coaches to conduct an off-site Life Planning experience.

4. *Give everyone a copy of the book.* You would probably expect us to say this, but we really believe in the power of books to spread ideas. We've tried to keep this one relatively brief and to the point. Our hope is that even nonreaders

will start and finish it. Bulk discounts are available directly from the publisher in both print and digital editions. We especially encourage you to do this in conjunction with a training experience as outlined in point 3 above.

5. *Offer employees additional paid time off.* Some companies give employees an entire day off to work on their Life Plan. The advantage of this is it really takes away the excuse that the employee doesn't have the time. A possible disadvantage is that he or she won't have any skin in the game. If you go with this option, we encourage you to build some kind of accountability into the process. It could be as simple as a form they sign indicating they completed the Life Planning process. It could also require that an accountability partner of their choosing cosign it. Regardless, few people abuse the privilege of having time off to complete their Life Plan. In our experience most employees are genuinely grateful and take the day seriously.

Other companies have offered a hybrid system where the company contributes a half day of paid time off and the employee uses a half day of their existing paid time off. The advantage is they then have skin in the game. The disadvantage is that this can be a little more complicated to administer and you are likely to get fewer takers.

We suggest you test your plan with a pilot group to gain insights into what works best in your culture. Once you eliminate the bugs, you can then roll it out to more departments or even company-wide.

6. *Provide encouragement and support.* This is perhaps the most important step. What happens *after* people develop a Life Plan is critically important. Having and living a Life Plan are two different things. The goal is not simply to create a document, put it into a file, and forget about it. The goal is

happy, productive employees who are pursuing passion and progress in every area of their lives.

You can provide ongoing encouragement and support in several ways:

- Appoint a Life Planning steering committee to roll out the process.
- Highlight success stories in your company newsletter, company-wide meetings, and other public venues.
- Set up a system of support groups, much like Weight Watchers does, with voluntary weekly or biweekly meetings.
- Build the Life Plan day into your employee benefits handbook and guide all new hires through the process.
- Build a video library of tips and Life Plan testimonials from your team.
- Schedule a regular time for your team to review their Life Plans and get coaching.

7. *Consider offering additional life resources.* To really see progress in their life accounts, people need motivation, education, and training. You might decide to provide these as a part of a larger life curriculum. For example, many companies make Weight Watchers, gym memberships, or similar programs available to their employees as a way of raising the overall health of the workforce. At Building Champions, for instance, we partner with the teammates in our corporate office to encourage them to use the gym or participate in our healthy food plan.

Several of our clients have brought in Dave Ramsey's *Financial Peace* program to help employees get out of debt and experience financial freedom. This often has a dramatic and almost immediate impact on people's productivity at work. Many feel for the first time that they are making financial progress and their work plays a key role in that.

Others have brought in various marriage training programs, like Gary Chapman's *The Five Love Languages*. These have the added advantage of directly involving spouses. Building Champions and several of its clients have had great success by inviting teammates to marriage retreats either created by us or conducted by other organizations with this expertise. Some companies have brought in parenting programs like Foster Cline and Jim Fay's *Parenting with Love and Logic*. Attention to family-related areas like these can also have a positive impact on work productivity.

The main thing is viewing this as something that is part of an ongoing program. Life Planning provides the foundation, but people need additional resources if they are really going to succeed.

What We're Really After

This may sound grandiose, but we are out to change the world. If you have made it this far in the book, we believe you share our goal. But we all know this change won't come because of new political initiatives, scientific or technological advances, or better or more accessible education. All of these might play a role, but none of them are enough.

Real transformation happens when people take responsibility for their own lives and begin to live intentionally in every area. When they begin recovering their passion and start seeing progress, their lives change. Changed people result in changed families, schools, synagogues, churches, companies, and governments. And when this happens, you begin transforming culture in profound and lasting ways.

So, as this book draws to a close, we invite you to help us launch a Life Planning revolution. We want to help people experience the difference a little planning and initiative can make—for them, their loved ones, and everything they hold dear.

Will you join us? The Living Forward revolution begins *with you.*

Conclusion

The Choice Is Yours

Let us endeavor so to live that when we come to die even the undertaker will be sorry.

—Mark Twain

You have come to a critical juncture in your Life Plan journey. You know what you need to know. We have given you the inspiration, training, and tools you need to create your own Plan. But ultimately, the choice is yours.

You can continue to drift and take your chances. As we saw in chapter 1, the odds are not in your favor. Without a Life Plan, you most likely end up far from where you hoped to be, regretting the decisions or inaction that shape your life. Or you can roll up your sleeves and get serious about this gift called Life. The choice is yours.

We're reminded of a story we heard about a wise old man who lived high in the Himalayan mountains. Periodically he ventured down into the local town to entertain the villagers with his special knowledge and talents. One of his skills was to psychically tell them the contents in their pockets, boxes, or minds.

A few young boys decided to play a joke on the old man and discredit his special abilities. One came up with the idea to capture a bird and hide it in his hands. He knew, of course, the man would know the object in his hands was a bird.

The boy devised a plan. Knowing the wise old man would correctly state the object in his hands was a bird, the boy would ask the old man if the bird was dead or alive. If the wise man said the bird was alive, the boy would crush the bird in his hands, so that when he opened his hands the bird would be dead. But if the man said the bird was dead, the boy would open his hands and let the bird fly free. No matter what the man said, the boy would prove the old man a fraud.

The following week, the man came down from the mountain into the village. The boy quickly caught a bird, cupped it out of sight behind his back, walked up to the wise old man, and asked, "What is it that I have in my hands?"

The man said, "You have a bird, my son."

The boy then asked, "Tell me, is the bird alive or dead?"

The wise old man looked at the boy and said, "The bird is as you choose it to be."

So it is with your life. The power is in your hands. You have been given a great gift—your life. What will you do with it?

Acknowledgments

This book would never have happened had it not been for the dedication of people, directly and indirectly, who contributed to its message. Though we are sure we will forget to mention many by name, we would especially like to thank the following people.

Michael acknowledges and thanks:

- My wife, Gail, for being my life partner for thirty-seven years. She is always quick to believe the best and forget the worst. She is the first person I want to see every morning and the last person I want to see every night. I love her more than words can convey.
- My five daughters and (so far) four sons-in-law, who bring such joy and fullness to my life. I am so proud of what each of them have accomplished in both winning at work and succeeding at life.
- My dad and mom, who now live nearby. Though they are in their eighties, I never hear them complain about

159

anything. They are two of the most positive, encouraging people I know. They provided everything I needed to become the man I have become.

- My teammates at Intentional Leadership, LLC, including Suzie Barbour, Andrew Buckman, Chad Cannon, Kyle Chowning, Sylvette Gannon, Madeline Lemon, Stu McLaren, Megan Miller, Joel Miller, Suzanne Norman, Raquel Newman, Mandi Rivieccio, Danielle Rodgers, and Brandon Triola. Their commitment to pursue what matters most inspires me every single day. They have allowed me to focus on what I do best, while they handle the rest.

- My coaches who have taught me how to create extraordinary outcomes for my life and work, including Daniel Harkavy, Dan Meub, Ilene Muething, Dan Sullivan, and Tony Robbins. You have shaped my thinking more than you know.

- My dear friends, Ken and Diane Davis, who allowed me to spend a month at their cabin in the Colorado Rockies, so I could bang out the first draft of this book. This book would not have happened without their generosity.

- Finally, I'd like to thank my dear friend, Daniel Harkavy, who first taught me about life planning, coached me through the process, and held me accountable for the results. He is a living testimony to the power of a life lived on purpose.

Daniel acknowledges and thanks:

- Sheri, my beautiful bride of twenty-seven years. You have been my "one" since I first laid eyes on you at the age of eleven! You have been my biggest cheerleader, my closest friend, and the one who so wonderfully completes me. Thank you for always encouraging me to live my Life Plan. SHMILY.

- My kids, Ali, Dylan, Wesley, and Emily. You guys make life so rich and fun! It has been such a blessing to be your dad and to now have you as our very close friends! I so love you and am so proud of who you are!

- All of the additional kids that have camped out at our place. Sharing life, meals, and adventures with you has been awesome!

- My parents Mel, Lynne, and my second mom/mother-in-law Gloria and all of our sibs and their fantastic kids. May you never underestimate how much I love and appreciate you.

- To my amazing executive assistant and second brain, Lynne Brown. How you serve and help me to lead well and live my Life Plan is huge. You are such a difference maker, and the Harkavy family is so grateful for you!

- The entire Building Champions team. Each and every one of you play a significant role in the work we do. You have contributed to this book's message as you have walked our many clients through this process over the past two decades. It is a joy to get to do this with you! Thank you, Todd Mosetter, for the work you did on this book. You helped me to make it better.

- Our thousands of Building Champions clients and friends who have gone through this process and helped to validate the impact Living Forward and Life Planning can have in one's life.

- The first guy to introduce the concept of Life Planning to me, my friend Todd Duncan. Thanks for sharing this life-changing gift with me!
- And finally, I would like to thank my friend and partner on this project, Michael Hyatt. Your humble heart, voracious appetite to grow, and your incredibly abundant spirit have made working on this project a wonderful experience.

And finally, we thank:

- Joel Miller, our researcher and editor on this project. He worked tirelessly on the manuscript, knitting our voices together into one seamless whole. We could not have finished this project without him.
- Our literary agents, Rick Christian and Bryan Norman of Alive Communications, who believed in this project from the get-go and helped find a publisher who shared our vision.
- Our acquisitions editor, Chad Allen; copyeditor, Barb Barnes; and the entire Baker Books team who have believed in this project and worked with us like true partners.

Our hope is that this message and process positively impacts many!

Life Planner's Quick Guide

Are you ready to dedicate a day to building your Life Plan? That's a major commitment, and to help you make the most of that time, we've created this Life Planner's Quick Guide to refresh you on all the major points and maintain positive momentum as you go.

Helpful Pointers

Block the day on your calendar and let everyone important—wife, boss, whoever—know that you're going to be out of pocket. Choose a suitable location, take everything you need to write and stay focused, and determine to go offline.

As you get started, remember to stay in a positive frame of mind. You're charting a course to your envisioned future. This is a time to be grateful, eager, and open. Trust the process and listen to your heart. There are no right or wrong answers. All you need to do is think, imagine, and write about something you care deeply about: *your life*.

The rest is as simple as following these five clearly marked steps.

Step 1: Write Your Eulogy

The first step in life planning is to consider where you want to end up. Nobody plans a trip without choosing a destination. For us that means writing your own eulogy. What will your legacy be? What will your life mean to those closest to you? What will they remember about you? How will your life have impacted theirs?

It might feel daunting, but this first step is critical. It will not only get your head in the game but also your heart. One easy way to begin is to list all the people you want to remember you: spouse, family members, friends, teammates, and so on. Then list how you want to be remembered by each of them: loyal, brave, kind, always eager to help—however you most desire to be remembered.

Once you have those elements, you can shape them into your eulogy. To see how others have done it, you can jump ahead to the Life Plan examples in the next section. The key is to write it as if your funeral is being held today, not some date down the road. By writing as if your eulogy was being delivered right now, you can begin thinking of what it will take to make those imagined memories real.

Step 2: Establish Your Life Accounts

Since you've written your eulogy, you already have a start on this. How and by whom you want to be remembered should begin to inform what Life Accounts you establish.

Here are some broad categories to work with: Spiritual, Marital, Parental, Social, Financial, and Personal. You can see a more thorough list and how the accounts might take shape on pages 72–76. You can have as few as five and as many as twelve. Most people end up with about nine. A starter list might look like this:

- You
- Faith
- Health
- Spouse
- Kids

- Finances
- Friends
- Work
- Hobbies

You should personalize and customize your list so it works well for you.

Step 3: Determine the Condition of Your Accounts

Think of your Life Accounts as bank accounts. What's the balance in each? Do you have what you need in each, or are you running low? Are you, for instance, overinvested in work and underfunding family? That's a typical problem, and this step is designed to identify those issues across all your accounts.

Step 4: Prioritize Your Life Accounts

We all have priorities. But we're not always clear on what they are, right? It's critical that we decide what accounts matter most so we can let them determine our actions. Where does work really fit in the scheme of things, your family, your friends, your community, your church? When we're not clear on what matters most, it's easy to give our attention to what simply demands the most.

And here's a tip. We explain this on pages 81–85, but it can be really helpful to put you and your self-care near the top. It's too easy to neglect what makes everything else possible.

Step 5: Fill Out Each Account

The most effective way to work with your Life Accounts is to create an Action Plan for each one. These five sections will help you get from where you are right now to where you want to be in each of these key areas of your life:

1. Draft a purpose statement that identifies your role and responsibility in this account.
2. Envision a future in which this account is in the black. Use the present tense and write down what that looks like.
3. Include an inspiring quote or verse that helps you connect emotionally with your purpose and the future you've envisioned.
4. State your current reality—good, bad, or ugly. The more honest you are, the easier it is to see what needs to change.
5. Finally, make specific commitments that detail the actions you need to take to get from your current reality to your envisioned future.

On this last point, be SMART—make sure you're not only specific, but that your commitments are also measurable, actionable, realistic, and time-bound. You want to dial these in so tight you can drop them onto your calendar or tomorrow's to-do list.

Remember, thousands of people have already created their Life Plans and are reaping the rewards. You can too. Check the next section for a few helpful examples.

————————

Visit our website at LivingForwardBook.com for the following resources:

- Life Assessment Profile
- Life Plan templates
- Ideal Week tool
- Annual Time Block tool
- Life Plan examples
- And more

Life Plan Examples

It's always easier to do something new if you can see someone else do it first. We wanted to do that for you here and bring together four different life plans from Building Champions clients. As you read, you'll get a sense of their individual lives and hopes, plus the various challenges they're all facing.

Each one is a little different—and not just in the particulars of their lives. Everyone builds their plan to fit their needs, going into as much detail and following the format as much as they think is necessary. Some are long. Some are short. Some are in between. They're all from men and women at different life stages and places in their careers.

They have their own unique outlooks and approaches to life—but they also have something in common. They all know that living intentionally is the most effective way to experience the kind of life they desire. As with many of the previous examples in the book, we've changed the names and details to protect people's privacy. We've also edited these for consistency and style, but we've tried to let their unique character shine through.

Hopefully, you'll find not only additional direction in these five examples but also freedom to build your plan to fit your life.

We have many more examples in our Life Plan Gallery at LivingForwardBook.com. You can even search to find those plans that most closely match your own situation.

———— Tom ————

Eulogy

Date of Birth: March 5, 1968
Date of Death: March 6, 2068

Tom was known as a family man whose mission in life was to positively impact the lives of children. He and his wife, Lisa, made their children, grandchildren, and great-grandchildren priorities in their lives. Lisa was the love of his life, and they spent many days together in love and laughter, both as a couple and with their amazing family.

Tom's three children had him wrapped around their respective fingers from the day they were born. He coached many of their basketball and baseball teams when they were younger, always emphasizing the same lessons: have fun, hustle, and display good sportsmanship. His kids never forgot those lessons and realized they were applicable not only in sports but in life: have fun, work hard, and treat others with kindness and respect.

After a lengthy career in the mortgage industry—including twenty years as the owner of a thriving mortgage company—Tom became a successful high-school basketball coach. Hundreds of the players he coached were in attendance at his memorial service, primarily because he cared more about them as people than as athletes.

The term *life balance* is one that Tom believed in wholeheartedly. He strived to instill the importance of balance into everyone he met, and his life was an example for others to follow.

Action Plans

Account 1: Lisa

Purpose:

I have an incredible life partner in Lisa. She is beautiful, thoughtful, understanding, smart, funny, athletic, and a lover of sports. Contributing to her happiness, success, and achievements brings me an incredible amount of joy. We work together to build a strong, happy, purposeful family.

Long-Term Vision:

Lisa and I will continue to date each other on a regular basis now and when we are empty nesters. We will continue working as a team toward goals and dreams, as well as enhancing our day-to-day happiness. We will continue to have a loving, passionate marriage that is able to withstand any turbulence.

Short-Term Goals/Specific Commitments:

1. I will devote at least two nights per month as "date nights" with Lisa. This evening will be spent without the kids.

2. I will spend "quiet time" (glass of wine, cuddling, etc.) with Lisa at least three times per week.

3. My family and I will take at least five vacations (overnight or more) outside our hometown each year.

4. My family and I will have one crazy-fun experience each quarter.

Account 2: Sarah, Sam, and Johnny

Purpose:

I have been given the most amazing gifts on Earth. Our kids rock! I will do everything possible to love and nurture Sarah, Sam, and Johnny and ensure that they grow up in a safe, fun, positive, and healthy environment.

Long-Term Vision:

I will have great relationships with my kids. They will be physically and emotionally healthy and happy, and they will contribute positively to my life, Lisa's life, and most importantly, society.

Short-Term Goals/Specific Commitments:

1. I will continue to coach each kid's baseball and basketball teams. I will spend one day/week in school with Johnny.
2. I will read three books and/or attend three clinics per year related to child development issues, motivating kids, coaching, etc.
3. I will have one date night (one-on-one time outside the house) each month with Sarah, Sam, and Johnny.
4. I will spend the day one-on-one with each child on their half-birthday, engaging in activities chosen by the kids.

Account 3: Physical Health

Purpose:

I am in excellent overall physical condition. My diet and exercise program have been carefully scrutinized. I eat foods, exercise, and sleep in a manner that contributes to a long, healthy life and gives me the necessary energy throughout the day that allows me to be a great husband, father, leader, and friend.

Long-Term Vision:

I will continue to monitor my health on an ongoing basis. I will be able to perform the same physical activities at fifty that I am able to perform at forty. My annual physical checkups show great results. I complete an Ironman Triathlon annually.

Short-Term Goals/Specific Commitments:

1. Work out at least seven times per week.
2. I will complete an Ironman Triathlon by 2013.
3. Each year I will have my diet and health evaluated by a health professional.
4. I will be in bed by 10:30 each night.

Account 4: Professional Success

Purpose:

My achievements in the professional world allow my family to obtain financial security and allow me to act as a mentor and leader to all my employees.

Long-Term Vision:

By forty-seven, I will have the ability to sell my company (most likely to my employees) for at least $3 million. I will be able to choose to devote my working hours to contributing to the lives of children.

Short-Term Goals/Specific Commitments:

1. I will create a business vision, business plan, and recruiting/retention plan—and incorporate these ideas into my daily activities.
2. I will make myself completely available to all employees for questions, coaching, deal structuring, etc.
3. I will read twelve books per year devoted to business-related topics.

Account 5: Financial Security

Purpose:

I will achieve financial freedom at the age of forty-seven, allowing me to devote more time to contributing to the lives of my children, without worrying about the financial implications of that decision.

Long-Term Vision:

By forty-seven, my family and I will live in a home with an indoor basketball court. By forty-five, our net worth, not including my business, will be at least $2 million dollars; by forty-seven, our net worth will be at least $3 million.

Short-Term Goals/Specific Commitments:

1. Lisa and I will meet with our financial advisor on a semi-annual basis to review our financial strategies and make necessary adjustments.
2. I will calculate my family's net worth each December.
   - Our real estate net worth should increase by at least 10 percent each year (from appreciation of properties and decrease in mortgage amounts owed).
   - Our equities plus cash (mutual funds, profit-sharing account, 401[k], checking accounts, etc.) net worth should increase by at least 10 percent each year (from added contributions and investment growth).

Account 6: Friendships

Purpose:

My friends have helped me through the highs and lows of my life. I have many great friendships, and I want to be able to contribute positively to my friends' lives.

Long-Term Vision:

I will continue to have close, dynamic, fun relationships with the people who are important in my family's life.

Short-Term Goals/Specific Commitments:

1. Each year my college friends will gather for a minimum of a three-day vacation.
2. Once each month we'll either invite friends over to our home for poker parties, kids' play dates, dinner, etc., or Lisa and I will go to dinner with them.

Account 7: Family

Purpose:

My parents are amazing people, and I will continue to love and support them, as they do me.

Long-Term Vision:

I will be very close with both of my parents, stepparents, and Lisa's family, visiting with them often.

Short-Term Goals/Specific Commitments:

1. I will plan one activity (lunch, dinner, etc.) every two months with my mom.
2. I will talk to my dad on the phone once per month.

———— **Rachel** ————

Eulogy

Rachel is absolutely the sweetest person I have ever met. She always had a smile on her face and had such a positive outlook on life. Since she was a little girl, Rachel had spunk about her that wouldn't quit. Her "overachiever syndrome" was evident from an early age and was further corroborated when she was selected as Most Likely to Succeed of her high-school senior class. Eager to get out into the educational workforce, she completed her undergraduate degree in only three years and graduated with her MSE plus 30 shortly thereafter.

Rachel was a phenomenal educator. She *loved* her students with her entire being and tirelessly poured into their development. She structured her classroom as a safe learning environment where her students felt worth within their classroom community. She later served in administration roles both as an instructional technology director and assistant principal in order to broaden her impact on student achievement. Even years later, she stayed connected with former students and continued to pour into them.

Rachel excelled in making others feel worth and dignity and made all who encountered her feel as if they could conquer the world. Through building relationships, she developed a strong and loyal customer base, many of whom became personal friends and valued her as a true partner and colleague.

Rachel excelled as an educational sales rep, never missing a given sales quota and always exceeding her given goal. She was passionate about education and strove to see children succeed! She was loyal to her customers and them to her. She was seen as a solid partner for schools and districts as well as a respected colleague.

There was a genuineness about Rachel that is not commonly found. She lit up a room when entering. Anyone she encountered was always glad to see her. She was sincere, encouraging, and had the kindest heart I knew.

Rachel's faith grounded and centered everything she did. Despite walking through difficulties, she maintained a positive outlook and firmly held to the fact that her Father was working for good on her behalf. She chose to use her pain and weaknesses to tirelessly pour into others. She was adamant her pain not be in vain and be used as a catalyst for growth in herself and others. Rachel lived in a constant state of improvement.

Her love for Jesus was also exemplified in the missions work she participated in over the course of her life. For as long as I remember, Rachel served in the local church in some capacity. In her thirties, after completing many mission trips domestically, she opened her heart to a country in Central America desperately needing the hope and love only Jesus can bring. Rachel fell in love with Guatemala and served many missions here.

Rachel loved her family. She was a daughter, sister, aunt, niece, and cousin and enjoyed spending any and all time she could with her family, whether close or distant. Her mom, Naomi, and her sister, Tanya, were truly her two best friends. She would have rather spent time with them than anyone else in the world. The three of them maintained a deep, close, and personal relationship.

In the little spare time she found, Rachel loved to play tennis and work in her yard. She found great joy in the outdoors and living in the sunshine. She was also an avid reader with a voracious desire to soak in new knowledge and information.

Rachel was truly a unique individual on many levels. It is a rarity to find someone so dedicated, so trustworthy, so caring, and so incredibly genuine.

—————— Action Plans ——————

Account 1: God

Envisioned Future:

I want to fully serve God, walking in his divine will and purpose. I want to be used magnificently to grow his kingdom and share his love and hope with others.

Purpose:

My purpose is to live my life in a way so there is no question of my faith or loyalty to my Savior. I want others to see him in me and know where my joy and hope lies. My purpose is to exude Jesus.

Specific Commitments:

- Spend a minimum of thirty minutes per day in quiet time and prayer.
- Read one spiritual book per month.
- Have continuous conversations with God throughout the day about anything and everything.
- Attend one Christ-centered conference per year.

Obstacles:

- A hectic schedule sometimes gets in the way of quality quiet time.
- Since I typically read at night, exhaustion sometimes replaces reading, and I choose to sleep.

Account 2: Me

Envisioned Future:

I am happy, living a life of freedom, flexibility, and service. I am continuously investing in myself and growing intellectually and spiritually while maintaining my mental and physical health.

Purpose:

My purpose is to live a positive and encouraging life displaying the love of Christ in every aspect.

Specific Commitments:

- Take one "unplugged" day per month.
- Continue coaching and development of my life plan to become the best me.
- Have quiet time on Sunday afternoons to relax and be at peace.
- Allow for two weekends a year for a trip alone to rest, recoup, and spend time with the Lord.
- Attend the 2015 World Domination Summit to be around like-minded, entrepreneurial people.

Obstacle:

- The largest obstacle to this account is overextending myself with work and personal commitments. More often than not, this account gets placed by the wayside and is not made a priority.

Account 3: Family

Envisioned Future:

I am a devoted daughter, taking care of my parents as they age. I owe them immensely for molding and shaping me into the person I am today. It is my heart's desire to spend as much quality time with them as possible, being available when needed to assist with life events. My siblings and their families are very much a part of my life, and I am also available to assist them physically, emotionally, etc. In addition, extended family also plays a big role in my life. I desire to be loyal and a support system for them when needed.

Purpose:

My purpose is to highly prioritize my family and their needs. Our time on Earth is limited and I will love my family well and deeply for the time I am blessed to have them.

Specific Commitments:

- Be more patient with my parents as they age, understanding they face and will face mental/health struggles.
- Take meaningful trips with my parents, providing for expenses they cannot afford.
- Spend one weekend a month with my parents (this will be hard until I can move closer).
- Spend two weekends a year with my sister at her home and trips together as our schedules allow.
- Text/talk with my brother and his wife. This is a huge step, as we have never communicated regularly. No reason why— just life has gotten in the way. I need to develop and build a solid relationship with both of them.
- Attend extended family events at least twice a year.
- Have consistent communication with extended relatives.

Obstacles:

- Lack of time
- Distance
- Coordination of schedules

Account 4: Service

Envisioned Future:

My service is not limited by full-time employment, and is only limited by the hours in the day. I am serving in the local church and community as well as internationally to spread the love and hope of Jesus.

Purpose:

My Father has immensely blessed me, and while I can never fully repay him for his goodness and mercy, my purpose is to share his love and hope with all I encounter.

Specific Commitments:

- Attend "Feed the Need" two Saturday nights a month.
- Serve in international missions at least twice a year.
- Host dinners in my home to bless others who are less fortunate, are down-and-out, or simply need encouragement.
- Actively seek out and pray about other opportunities to serve in the local church and community.

Obstacle:

- Retention of a full-time "employed" job will reduce the amount and quality of time I have to serve.

Account 5: Career

Envisioned Future:

I am self-employed, freeing me up to live a life of service that lends greater purpose for the kingdom. I blog, encouraging others who have walked a similar path, sharing the love and hope my Father has graciously showered upon me. I have multiple real-estate holdings which allow for passive income. As time allows, I travel nationally and internationally providing professional development opportunities for educators and also maintain an independent sales relationship with my current company. I also maintain a booth at an antique store where I sell repurposed/painted furniture and antiques.

Purpose:

My purpose is to earn income and fully support myself while being self-employed. This, in turn, will open me up for greater flexibility and opportunities for service and for growing his kingdom.

Specific Commitments:

- Become fully self-employed in 2015.
- Purchase one rental property in 2015.
- Begin blogging in 2015.
- Secure booth space in an antique store.
- Use industry connections to gain per diem work opportunities.

Obstacles:

- False sense of security of being employed full-time drives fear.
- Many opportunities and choices make it difficult to select a path.

Account 6: Personal Relationships

Envisioned Future:

While my span of relationships is very broad, I am a close and loyal friend to a small handful. I invest in others continuously, but I have a core group of friends that "sticks closer than a brother." I am trustworthy and dependable and available when my core group is in need.

Purpose:

My purpose is to develop deep, lasting, and godly relationships with a few very close friends.

Specific Commitments:

- Spend a minimum of one night a month with girlfriends.
- Take one annual girlfriends trip.
- Actively reach out to close friends to secure opportunities to pray and minister in their lives.
- Send notes of encouragement when appropriate.

Obstacles:

- I really like being alone, and it's often easier to relax than to put forth effort into getting ready and attending an event with a friend.
- I often have good intentions to reach out to a friend but get sidetracked or preoccupied.

Account 7: Financial

Envisioned Future:

I am completely debt-free. Because I was frugal and saved in my early working years, I have a retirement that is able to sustain me. I accept per diem work opportunities on a case-by-case basis. I have passive income being generated through rental properties and blogging. I continue to be a good steward of the resources my Father has lovingly and mercifully blessed me with. I give above and beyond the 10 percent that is required, while also investing in missionaries and other organizations. I don't desire to be "rich" or have things, but I desire to live comfortably and be able to spend time and money on experiences and philanthropic venues.

Purpose:

My purpose is to earn income, support myself, and continue to live a life free of debt. In addition, it is my purpose to earn income in order that I may give back to the local church and other faith-based organizations, therefore supporting the growth of the kingdom.

Specific Commitments:

- Max out retirement contributions annually.
- Read books (e.g., *Launch* by Jeff Walker, *The 4-Hour Work-week* by Timothy Ferriss) to discover and inspire new ways to generate passive income.
- Maintain a healthy standard of living while taking a large pay cut in exchange for a flexible schedule.

- Give away 20 percent or more of my income annually.
- Meet with a financial advisor to look at the full picture before transitioning into self-employment.

Obstacles:

- If self-employed and income is not steady, retirement and philanthropic contributions could dwindle.
- Unforeseen circumstances could arise, greatly affecting my stable financial situation. This thought sometimes drives fear.

Account 8: Physical Health

Envisioned Future:

I will maintain a healthy body weight and BMI, supported by a Paleo diet and daily exercise.

Purpose:

My body is his temple and my purpose is to keep it functioning for as long as possible so that I may effectively carry out his will and plan.

Specific Commitments:

- Walk ten or more miles per week.
- Play tennis two times per week.
- Eat a diet high in protein, fruits, and vegetables and low in carbs.
- Drink five to six bottles of water each day or the equivalent.
- Wear sunscreen if I'm outside for an extended period of time.

Obstacles:

- Travel sometimes prevents me from eating healthy, exercising, and drinking water like I should.
- Lack of time and energy prevents me from playing tennis.

Account 9: Hobbies and Travel

Envisioned Future:

I have a full life that includes opportunities for travel and leisure. I travel nationally and internationally to experience the wonders the Lord has provided. I am experiencing new cultures that allow for a greater appreciation of life.

Purpose:

My purpose is to live a rich, full, and culturally diverse life with an appreciation for simplicity.

Specific Commitments:

• Play tennis twice a week.
• Read one to three books per month.
• Travel internationally two to three times per year at minimum for missions and leisure.
• Visit three or more new places in the US each year.
• Maintain a lush, rich, and colorful yard.

Obstacle(s):

• Hobbies often take a back burner to other work and personal commitments.
• Full-time employment/lack of vacation days prevents me from traveling as I wish.

———— Angela ————

Outcomes

How I want to be remembered by those closest to me:

- Grace: Being there when it mattered and loving her with every ounce of myself.
- Mom and Stepdad: Always doing what's right.
- Timothy: Putting Grace above our issues.
- Kate: Being there, having fun, and caring.
- My team at work: Being supportive and dependable.
- Frank: Being there when he needed me. Being a role model.

Eulogy

Here lies Angela. She was loved by her daughter, Grace, and parents, June and David. She had a long, successful career in mortgage lending. Starting at the early age of nineteen, she worked her way from an entry-level processor to a regional processing manager for all of Colorado. Her hard work and dedication were felt by all she supported at the bank. That same hard work and dedication was an anthem throughout Angela's life, and everything she did was with total determination.

Although you'd never know it, Angela always felt as though she had only a few friends. But she was always there for them and for many good times. She shared time camping, hiking, exercising, and drinking cocktails, as well as the occasional John Hiatt concert. She was the one person you could count on to be 100 percent honest and to always persevere. Any time she fell down (which happened a lot on stairs), she would pick herself right back up.

Her greatest love and accomplishment is her daughter, Grace. She always pushed her to be the best and taught her to be strong and independent, just like her mother. She is the legacy of her mother, and Angela was so proud of that Great Accomplishment. Grace, you were so loved!

——————— Action Plans ———————

Account 1: Grace

Envisioned Future:

Today we leave for Hawaii. Grace just graduated from college and we are celebrating her accomplishments. Going to our favorite spot. I'm so glad she has such a nice boyfriend who totally gets our Grace-Mom time and is okay with our being away a week. He totally appreciates her independent spirit. She starts her internship in a couple of weeks, so a relaxing time in Hawaii will be perfect. We will have so much fun snorkeling, shopping, and just hanging out by the pool. Oh, and don't forget hiking! It's so great we enjoy doing things together.

Purpose:

To make sure Grace knows she is my priority and to enjoy our time spent together.

Specific Commitments:

1. Mommy and Grace day: One day a month where we only do stuff with just her and me. Frequency: Monthly.
2. Be on time: Be on time when picking her up or going to an event. Frequency: As needed.
3. Daily check-in: Check how day was, complete reading log, check homework, violin practice. Frequency: Daily.

Account 2: Health

Envisioned Future:

We are super excited about this Hawaii trip! Today we are going on a full-day hike and then a swim when we get back. It's so nice to be almost fifty and look good in a bathing suit and have the energy to hike the falls. It's so beautiful to see the cascading waterfalls, towering bamboo, and huge rain forest. Heaven!

Purpose:

To be physically fit enough to enjoy all life has to offer, especially the outdoors, and to feel good in whatever I choose to wear.

Specific Commitments:

1. Boot camp: Go to boot camp to exercise for one hour. Frequency: Five days a week.
2. Physical activity: Hiking, swimming, biking, or other outdoor activity. Frequency: Biweekly.
3. Nutrition: Eat healthier whole food, including fruits, veggies, and lean proteins. Be disciplined and plan ahead. Frequency: Daily.

Account 3: Finances

Purpose:

To regularly save money to have financial reserves, as well as accomplish short-term goals.

Specific Commitments:

1. Save money. Put $500 into accounts that are not used or readily accessible. Frequency: Monthly.
2. Increase 401(k). Make an increase in the amount of money put into my 401(k). Frequency: Monthly.
3. Curb spending. Be more deliberate about how and when I spend my money (and make lists when shopping). Frequency: Daily.

Account 4: Home

Purpose:

To take more pride in my home and enjoy being there.

Specific Commitments:

1. Straighten up: Wash dishes and put away clutter that collects downstairs. Frequency: Every other day.
2. Clean bathrooms and floors: Clean bathtubs, toilets, sinks, and floors. Vacuum floors and mop. Frequency: Biweekly.
3. Laundry: Do one load of laundry. Wash, dry, and put away. Frequency: Daily.
4. Clean garage: Clean out garage, donate junk, and throw out trash. Frequency: Quarterly.

Account 5: Friends

Purpose:

To forge stronger bonds with the friends I have and build new relationships.

Specific Commitments:

1. Reach out: Reach out to one to two friends by phone, email, or Facebook. Frequency: Daily.
2. Make plans: Make plans to visit with a friend for lunch, dinner, or other activity. Frequency: Biweekly.
3. Random act: Send or deliver a random act of kindness. Frequency: Monthly.

Account 6: Fun

Purpose:

To get out and enjoy life as an adult, both with and without my child.

Specific Commitments:

1. Get outside: Go for a walk or hike for twenty to thirty minutes at least. Frequency: Weekly.

2. Try something new. Do an activity that I have never done (e.g., take a class or volunteer). Frequency: Quarterly.
3. Start a book club: Find a few people who would like to start a book club. Frequency: Monthly.
4. Camp: Take RV out to camp. Frequency: Monthly.
5. See #2 from Account 5.

——————— **Scott** ———————

Outcomes

By whom do I want to be remembered?
• God
• My wife, Catherine
• Our children: Mark, Seth, and Nick (and their future spouses and family)
• Our family
• Our friends
• My co-workers
• Industry peers and acquaintances

What will they remember about me?
• Through my actions, real evidence that Jesus Christ is my personal Lord and Savior.
• My lifelong marriage commitment with Catherine.
• My family-first commitment and unconditional love for all family members.
• My passion for discovering and living out God's plan through a purpose-driven life.
• My passion for enjoying life and sharing life's experiences with family and friends.
• That by prayerfully seeking God's will and his plan, I added positive value to God's kingdom and to my family, co-workers, friends, and industry peers.
• A loving, caring, kind, generous, and helpful attitude.
• Being a man of high integrity, honesty, and optimism.

- My commitment to excellence in all endeavors.
- That I operated with a servant-leader mentality ("You can achieve whatever you want in life if you help enough other people get what they want").
- My belief that every experience, whether good or bad, specifically prepares you for God's unique plan for your life.
- My daily prayer asking God to open the doors we should enter and explore, and shut the doors we should avoid.

—————— **Action Plans** ——————

Account 1: God

Envisioned Future:

I want to be closer to God and, through daily Bible study and prayer, understand and passionately pursue his purpose for me. I know God has a specific plan for me, and I want to accomplish all that he wants of me, so my life has eternal meaning and purpose. I want my life to add lasting positive value to his kingdom and to my family, friends, co-workers, and peers.

Purpose:

I will be a Christian example, with a meaningful, purpose-driven life, providing inspiration to my family members and others to use their God-given talents to seek excellence in their chosen endeavors while making a positive difference in the lives of the people they touch.

Specific Commitments:

- Daily morning prayer and quiet time.
- Personal Bible study/devotional before bedtime.
- Weekly group Bible study.
- Attend church regularly.
- Two personal days a year for reflection and update of My Life Plan (June, December).

Account 2: Catherine

Envisioned Future:

Catherine will be my very best friend, traveling companion, and lover. Together we will fill our memory bank to the brim with joyful times, shared adventures, close family relationships, and close friendships. We must continue our important roles of parenting and mentoring our children. Together, we will always be there to support our family and friends in time of need.

Purpose:

God chose Catherine to be my lifelong companion and me to be Catherine's companion. Two people acting as one, unified with shared purpose, goals, and convictions, create an inseparable bond for a solid foundation for happiness and family cohesiveness.

Specific Commitments:

- Take trips together and enjoy new experiences away from home.
- Include Catherine on business trips and Masters Coach events.
- Initiate daily contact by phone to see how Catherine's day is going.
- Get home by 5 p.m. at least one day a week.
- Have occasional lunch or breakfast with Catherine in the city.
- Take a monthly excursion together for shopping, sightseeing, etc.
- Give occasional surprise flowers, gifts, fun items.
- Make evening time together for dates or hot tub or fire-pit visits.

Account 3: Children

Envisioned Future:

Our children and their families and friends will enjoy spending time with us, and our family relationships will grow even stronger, more enjoyable, and more intimate after each encounter. They will learn important Christian family values and business ethics from us, and they will create strong, stable, caring families of their own. They will honor God by living meaningful, purpose-driven lives that will add value to God's kingdom.

Purpose:

It's my responsibility to mentor our children, teaching them Christian values; and it's my prayer that our family seeds forever will all worship Jesus Christ as their personal Lord and Savior and seek Jesus to be their life guide. This would be our greatest legacy.

Specific Commitments:

- Initiate personal contact multiple times weekly.
- Always be available to listen to their needs and concerns.
- Have personal, one-on-one time monthly.
- Have family gatherings monthly.
- Spend Christmas and Thanksgiving together, at home or on a trip.
- Unconditionally love their future spouses and in-laws and openly welcome them as part of our family.

Account 4: Other Family Members

Envisioned Future:

I want my family members to understand that I am available to help them through good times and bad times, whether spiritually, physically, or financially.

Purpose:

My role is to stay in touch, offer my help, organize the activities we can share together, and be a willing mentor; and to demonstrate to my children the importance of family.

Specific Commitments:
- Call Mom multiple times a week and visit her often.
- Include family members in some of our activities.
- Send notes/emails to nieces and nephews for them to use me as a "sounding board."
- Extend invitations to the Ranch.

Account 5: Close Friends

Envisioned Future:

Catherine and I will develop close friendships so we can enjoy and share times with our friends, and provide mutual support to each other's families.

Purpose:

Friendships outside our family are important for enjoying and sharing life's experiences, but also for the development of family support teams.

Specific Commitments:
- Movie nights and dinners together weekly.
- Quarterly wine/pool/spa parties, "Men's Night Out" for poker, golf, lake house.
- Trips with friends.

Account 6: Health and Fitness

Envisioned Future:

I will be physically fit and maintain a weight under 225 pounds throughout my life, being an example for my children to encourage them to maintain healthy lifestyles throughout their lives.

Purpose:

In order to accomplish my Life Plan, my dreams, and my goals and to enjoy Catherine, my family, and my friends, I must remain healthy.

Specific Commitments:

- Weight goals must be set and monitored.
- Daily cardiovascular and strength training (minimum of thirty minutes, four days a week).
- Semiannual dental exams.
- Annual physical exams.
- Colonoscopy exams as recommended by doctor.

Account 7: Wealth Preservation and Management

Envisioned Future:

Catherine and I will accumulate assets that will provide a safe investment income stream of $100,000 pretax monthly, without withdrawing capital.

Purpose:

Our investment income provides Catherine and me the necessary funds to achieve our goals involving family, friends, business strategies, good health, recreation, travel, and charitable causes.

Specific Commitments:

- Prepare a monthly balance sheet with detailed accounts.
- Utilize sound investment principles.
- Transfer property ownership to family limited partnerships.
- Update family wealth strategy and wills.

Account 8: Successful Business

Envisioned Future:

Lead my company as a high-integrity, family-oriented, Christian-based company and pursue its vision of using our God-given talents to make a positive contribution to the lives of our employees, shareholders, customers, and the people who provide services to us.

Purpose:

My business is the vehicle or pulpit to help me accomplish my Life Plan and make a positive difference in people's lives.

Specific Commitments:

- Support, explain, preach, and live out our vision statement.
- Connect with the hearts of our people.
- Constantly look for ways to add value to our people and our customers.
- Develop Life Plans for interested employees.
- Implement a phantom stock ownership plan for key people.
- Establish and distribute realistic corporate goals.
- Hold regional managers and direct reports accountable for results.
- Develop the lending industry's most respected sales training and coaching team.
- Publish an article or write a book of inspiration.
- Take two days off annually to discuss strategy and goals (May and Dec.).

Account 9: Recreation and Travel

Envisioned Future:

Catherine and I will have active lifestyles involving many activities, including travel, golf, hunting, fishing, boating, and skiing with close friends and family members.

Purpose:

To enjoy life and experience the beauty of God's earth.

Specific Commitments:

- Build several venues for family fun and travel.
- Build a legacy home on a crystal clear river that my children and grandchildren will never want to sell.
- Take frequent outings with family and friends.
- Take annual fishing trips.
- Take annual hunting trips.
- Take annual golf trips.
- Fulfill travel list:
  - Alaska (2010 with Nick)
  - Scotland, Ireland (with kids)
  - Italy
  - The Holy Land (with kids)
  - Egypt and the Pyramids
  - Nantucket
  - The Cloisters at Sea Island
  - South Africa
  - Henry's Fork Lodge
  - New Zealand
  - China
  - Bali (Cottage on the bay)
  - Vancouver, Canada
  - Albany, Georgia (Sherwood Baptist Church)
- Bucket list activities:
  - Play Augusta National Golf Club
  - Catch a tarpon, bonefish, snook, and permit on a fly rod
  - Catch a peacock bass
  - Catch a largemouth bass over 10 pounds
  - Play the Old Course in Scotland
  - View the Northern Lights
  - Harvest a 170-plus-inch whitetail deer

Account 10: Charitable Giving

Envisioned Future:

Catherine and I will be good stewards of the monetary blessings God has provided us.

Purpose:

To give back to the church and community as part of our tithe.

Specific Commitments:

- My Mount Everest goal: Donate $5 million to charity.
- Give monthly to my local Christian radio station and other Christian-based organizations in an amount equal to 10 percent of our gross monthly income.

Notes

Chapter 2 Understand the Mission

1. Benjamin Franklin, *Autobiography of Benjamin Franklin*, ed. Frank Woodworth Pine (New York: Henry Holt and Co., 1922), chap. 9.
2. SWOT: acronym for a popular analytical tool to assess strengths, weakness, opportunities, threats.

Chapter 4 Design Your Legacy

1. Psalm 90:12 NIV.
2. Small business guru Michael Gerber recommends a similar exercise in *The E-Myth Revisited* (New York: HarperCollins, 1995), 129.
3. Eugene O'Kelly, *Chasing Daylight* (New York: McGraw-Hill, 2007), 110ff.

Chapter 5 Determine Your Priorities

1. William J. Bennett and David Wilezol, *Is College Worth It?* (Nashville: Thomas Nelson, 2013). Chapter 3 analyzes the ROI on several different majors and dozens of schools.

Chapter 6 Chart the Course

1. On the problem of fantasy: Christian Jarrett, "Why Positive Fantasies Make Your Dreams Less Likely to Come True," *BPS Research Digest*, May 25, 2011, http://digest.bps.org.uk/2011/05/why-positive-fantasies-make-your-dreams.html. Why envisioning works: Frank Niles, "How to Use Visualization to Achieve Your Goals," *Huffington Post*, August 17, 2011, http://www.huffingtonpost.com/frank -niles-phd/visualization-goals_b_878424.html. For an example of how our subconscious mind works on solving problems while we're focused on other things,

see Tom Stafford, "Your Subconscious Is Smarter Than You Might Think," BBC .com, February 18, 2015, http://www.bbc.com/future/story/20150217-how-smart -is-your-subconscious. See also Shlomit Friedman, "Priming Subconscious Goals," in *New Developments in Goal Setting and Task Performance*, eds. Edwin A. Locke and Gary P. Latham (New York: Routledge, 2013). On the connection between confidence regarding our goals and accomplishing them: Gabriele Oettingen, "Regulating Goal Pursuit through Mental Contrasting with Implementation Intentions," in Lock and Latham, *New Developments in Goal Setting and Task Performance*.

2. Contemporary adaptation is taken from Lawrence Pearsall Jacks, *Education through Recreation* (New York: Harper and Brothers, 1932), 1–2.

3. Proverbs 2:2 NASB.

4. Henry Cloud, *9 Things You Simply Must Do to Succeed in Love and Life* (Nashville: Thomas Nelson, 2004), 121–22.

Chapter 7 Dedicate One Day

1. Proverbs 20:5 NASB.

2. Steven Pressfield, *The War of Art* (New York: Warner Books, 2003).

Chapter 8 Implement Your Plan

1. Lydia Saad, "The '40-Hour' Workweek Is Actually Longer—by Seven Hours," Gallup.com, August 29, 2014, http://www.gallup.com/poll/175286/hour-work week-actually-longer-seven-hours.aspx. Jennifer J. Deal, "Always On, Never Done?" Center for Creative Leadership, August 2013, https://s3.amazonaws.com /s3.documentcloud.org/documents/1148838/always-on-never-done.pdf.

2. William Ury, *The Power of a Positive No* (New York: Bantam, 2007), 16.

3. You can find additional examples in a post Michael wrote called "Using E-mail Templates to Say No with Grace" at http://michaelhyatt.com/say-no-with -grace.html.

Chapter 9 Keep It Alive

1. David Allen, *Getting Things Done* (New York: Penguin, 2001), 184–85.

2. Ibid., 185–87.

3. For more on this topic, see Michael's post "The Lost Art of Note Taking" at http://michaelhyatt.com/recovering-the-lost-art-of-note-taking.html.

About the Authors

Michael Hyatt is the author of *Platform: Get Noticed in a Noisy World* (Thomas Nelson, 2012). It is a *New York Times*, *Wall Street Journal*, and *USA Today* bestseller. Recently, *Forbes* magazine named him one of the "Top 10 Online Marketing Experts to Follow in 2014."

Michael is the former chairman and CEO of Thomas Nelson Publishers, the largest faith-based publisher in the world and now part of HarperCollins. He began his career at Word Publishing while a senior at Baylor University. In the thirty-five years since then, he has worked in nearly every facet of book publishing.

He is also an expert in the field of social media. His blog, MichaelHyatt.com, is ranked by Google in the top one-half percent of all blogs with more than 450,000 unique visitors a month. He has readers in more than two hundred countries.

His podcast, *This Is Your Life*, is consistently in the Top Ten in the Business category on iTunes and downloaded by more than 300,000 people a month. He has more than 215,000 followers on Twitter. He has appeared on more than 100 television shows, including several on ABC, NBC, CBS, and CNN. He has also been on more than 1,000 syndicated and local radio shows.

Michael has been married to his wife, Gail, for thirty-five years. They have five daughters, four sons-in-law, and eight grandchildren. They live just outside of Nashville, Tennessee.

Over the past twenty-five years, **Daniel Harkavy** has coached thousands of business leaders to peak levels of performance, profitability, and fulfillment. In 1996, he harnassed his passion for coaching teams and leaders to found Building Champions, where he serves as CEO and executive coach. Today the company has nearly fifty employees, with a team of twenty executive and leadership coaches who provide guidance to thousands of clients and organizations. Some of the clients include Bank of America, Chick-fil-A, Daimler Trucks North America, MetLife, Pfizer, Infineum (an ExxonMobil and Shell company), US Bank, PrimeLending, Dale Carnegie Training, JPMorgan Chase, Keller Williams, Mary Kay, Morgan Stanley, Northwestern Mutual, Thomas Nelson, Wells Fargo, Century 21, and many others.

In 2007, Daniel authored *Becoming a Coaching Leader: The Proven Strategy for Building Your Own Team of Champions* (Nelson). Drawing upon years of experience, Daniel offered leaders a coaching system to more effectively develop teams and achieve lasting results.

Prior to Building Champions, Daniel spent ten years in the financial services industry, eight of which were focused on coaching and team development. His career in finance was fast-tracked after quickly developing his team into the company's most productive and profitable group. Daniel attributes his success to creating healthy and productive cultures.

Daniel lives in West Linn, Oergon, with his wife and family, where he actively serves his community as a member of nonprofit boards and a mentor to those seeking his advice. His other passions include surfing, snowboarding, and hanging out with his family.

Contact Michael and Daniel

To get the latest *Living Forward* updates and resources, visit LivingForwardBook.com.

Michael and Daniel speak frequently on the topic of Life Planning. They can deliver a keynote, half-day, or full-day version of this content, depending on your needs, either together or alone. For more information, please visit Living ForwardBook.com.

You can connect with Michael here:
- Email: michael@michaelhyatt.com
- Blog: http://michaelhyatt.com
- Twitter: http://twitter.com/michaelhyatt
- Facebook: http://facebook.com/michaelhyatt

You can connect with Daniel here:
- Email: daniel@buildingchampions.com
- Blog: http://buildingchampions.com
- Twitter: http://twitter.com/danielharkavy
- Facebook: http://facebook.com/danielharkavy

ONLINE TOOLKIT
TO MAKE IT ALL HAPPEN

Get everything you need to create and follow your Life Plan, including:

 Plug-and-play templates to help you build your personal Life Plan

Proven time management tools to help you stay ahead of your week and your year

Life Plan examples to inform and inspire your own

Start strong and finish well by visiting . . .

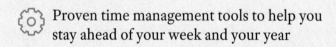

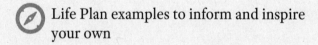 LivingForwardBook.com

GET WHERE YOU WANT TO BE
IN BUSINESS AND LIFE.

LET OUR TEAM OF COACHES
GUIDE YOU.

For more than twenty years, we've helped people improve the way they lead, live, and perform. Let us show you how.

 One-on-one coaching

 Speaking and keynotes

 Workshops and retreats

Contact us to start your journey.

BuildingChampions.com/LivingForward

503-906-2003

 BUILDING CHAMPIONS

PRODUCTIVITY
ISN'T ABOUT
GETTING MORE DONE.
IT'S ABOUT DOING WHAT YOU WANT.

If we don't control our calendars, someone else will—and that means less time to do what we want. In Michael's new online productivity course, *More Margin*, you'll discover:

- How to use the nine laws of productivity

- Why productivity depends mostly on what you don't do

- How to effectively eliminate, automate, and delegate your work

- One trick that will simultaneously increase both your efficiency and your free time

Find out how *More Margin* can help you free your calendar . . .

LivingForwardBook.com